Enjoying Good Health

Second Edition

Delores Shimmin

A Beka Book® Pensacola, FL 32523-9100
a ministry of PENSACOLA CHRISTIAN COLLEGE

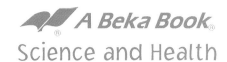

A Beka Book® Science and Health

Science		Health
God's World	K5	
Discovering God's World	1	Health, Safety, and Manners 1
Enjoying God's World	2	Health, Safety, and Manners 2
Exploring God's World	3	Health, Safety, and Manners 3
Understanding God's World	4	Developing Good Health
Investigating God's World	5	Enjoying Good Health
Observing God's World	6	Choosing Good Health
Science: Order and Reality	7	A Healthier You
Matter and Motion in God's Universe	8	Let's Be Healthy
Science of the Physical Creation	9	Health in Christian Perspective
Biology: God's Living Creation	10	Managing Your Life under God
Chemistry: Precision and Design	11	Sex, Love, and Romance *(Sex Education from the Bible)*
Physics: The Foundational Science	12	

9–12 (bracketing the 9, 10, 11 Health titles)

Enjoying Good Health
Second Edition

Staff Credits
Editor: Naomi Sleeth
Designer: Chris Martinez
Illustrators: Steven Haught, Chris Martinez, Grace Larson, Brian Jekel, Dan Cordova, Dan Olsen, Jonathan Taylor, Frank Hicks, Steven Hileman, John Ball

A Beka Book, a Christian textbook ministry of Pensacola Christian College, is designed to meet the need for Christian textbooks and teaching aids. The purpose of this publishing ministry is to help Christian schools reach children and young people for the Lord and train them in the Christian way of life.

Cataloging Data
Shimmin, Delores.
        Enjoying good health / Delores Shimmin—2nd edition
        p. : col. ill.; 28 cm. (A Beka Book health series)
    Includes Index
    1. Health education (Elementary) II. A Beka Book, Inc.
Library of Congress: RA 440. S25 E6 1999
Dewey System: 372.3

Contents

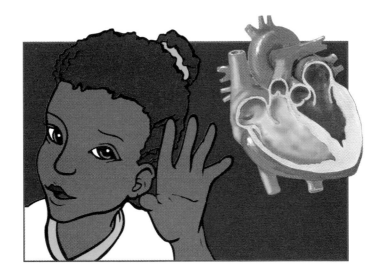

chapter 2 — Food for Vitality

chapter 3 — Your 30-foot-long Canal

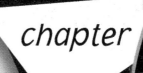

Your Transportation System

The intricate workings of our bodies point to God's wisdom in creation and cause us to exclaim with the Psalmist—"I will praise Thee; for I am fearfully and wonderfully made: marvelous are Thy works; and that my soul knoweth right well" (Ps. 139:14). Our bodies have thousands of parts which are carefully designed to perform hundreds of jobs. No man has been able to design a machine that can take in food or fuel and change it into other things the machine needs in order to grow, to repair itself, and to do work. Man designs machines, but only God can design a living person.

Parts
of the blood

White blood cells
fight infection.

Platelets
clot blood.

Red blood cells
carry oxygen.

Life in the blood

The Bible says that "the life of the flesh is in the blood" (Lev. 17:11). Your blood carries oxygen and nutrients to all parts of your body. The powerful muscle that keeps your blood constantly flowing is your heart, or **cardiac muscle.** This muscle pumps blood through thousands of miles of arteries, veins, and capillaries. **Arteries** carry blood *away from your heart* to tiny blood vessels called **capillaries,** the smallest vessels of your body. **Veins** collect the blood from the capillaries and return it *to the heart.*

Your body has *about three quarts of blood* traveling through it; an adult has about five quarts of blood. After food is digested, it is absorbed into the blood. *Food and oxygen are moved from one part of your body to another through the bloodstream.* Your blood also helps fight diseases, supplies water to your body, and collects waste products to be removed.

Over 50% of your blood is made up of *plasma*—the liquid part of the blood. One job of plasma is to carry digested food throughout your body. Blood also contains *red blood cells,* which carry oxygen; *white blood cells,* which fight infection and disease; *antibodies* [ăn′tĭ·bŏd′ēz], which fight pathogens (germs); and *platelets,* which help the blood to clot if a blood vessel (an artery, vein, or capillary) has been cut.

Plasma carries digested food

Plasma is a yellow or straw-colored liquid that is mostly water. Digested food is added to the plasma at the small intestine and taken to every part of the body. Waste materials are collected in the plasma and taken out by the lungs, kidneys, liver, and sweat glands. Plasma also helps fight infection and helps the blood to clot (thicken) and form a scab over a wound. **Antibodies,** which your body manufactures to help protect you from disease, are also found in the plasma.

Red cells carry oxygen

Iron is an important mineral which helps give the red blood cells their color. The reason your blood appears to be red is that every drop contains millions of red blood cells. The red blood cells absorb oxygen in your lungs and carry it throughout your body; after they give up the oxygen they carry, they look a bluish-red color. Then the red blood cells return to the lungs to pick up more oxygen. On their journey back, the red blood cells carry nearly one fourth of the carbon dioxide which is released at the air sacs. The rest of the carbon dioxide is dissolved in the plasma. When the dissolved carbon dioxide reaches the lungs, it is exhaled.

Remember that every part of your body needs oxygen to do its work. If there are not enough red blood cells to supply oxygen to the body, the whole body is weakened and slowed down. Every day, your body uses up about two ounces of blood. To replace the used red blood cells, your body requires iron. Most of your body's iron comes from old red blood cells which your liver recycles so that they can be used over and over. Your body needs additional iron, however, which can be obtained from foods that are rich in iron.

Good food sources of *iron* include *liver, lean meats, shellfish, dark green leafy vegetables, egg yolk, soybeans, dried peas and beans, dried fruits, whole-grain breads and cereals, wheat germ,* and *dark molasses.*

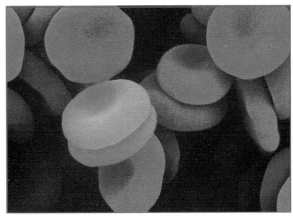
red blood cells

White cells fight infection

Blood contains fewer white cells than red cells, but the white blood cells are usually larger than the red cells. White blood cells are not swept along by the bloodstream as red blood cells are. Instead, they have the ability to move around by themselves.

The primary purpose of the white blood cells is to defend your body against disease. Whenever your skin is cut or punctured, allowing disease-causing viruses or bacteria to enter the bloodstream, your body's army of white blood cells is instantly called into action. Millions of them quickly surround and begin to destroy the pathogens. This action keeps the pathogens from spreading through your body. If you do not take proper care of your body by eating a variety of good foods and getting suffi-

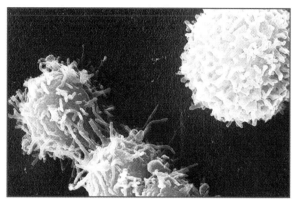
white blood cells

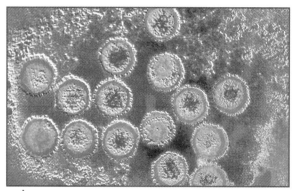
viruses

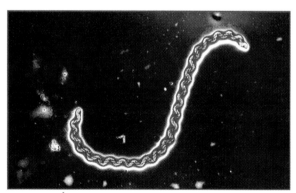
bacterium

Platelets cover open wounds

If a small blood vessel is cut or broken, tiny platelets in the blood stick to the rough edges of the wound and to each other. They pile up to form a temporary covering over the injury. The platelets also help the blood to clot. A blood clot on your skin—called a **scab**—prevents the wound from bleeding and helps keep the wound clean. If a cut does not stop bleeding, you should apply pressure on it with a clean cloth. If the pressure fails to stop the bleeding, the cut may need stitches in order to heal properly.

If the body does not have enough vitamin K, the blood will not clot properly, causing the body to lose too much blood from even a small cut or scratch. Most vitamin K is produced by bacteria in the colon. Eating *yogurt* which contains bacteria helps your body to produce this vitamin. *Green leafy vegetables* also provide your body with vitamin K.

cient rest and exercise, the white blood cells may not be able to prevent an infection or disease. Sometimes bacteria kill the white blood cells. When this happens, dead white blood cells gather at the place of infection, forming pus.

Quick Checkup
Who am I?

1. I move food and oxygen from one part of your body to another.
   bloodstream

2. I make up over half of your blood.
   plasma

3. We carry oxygen to every part of your body.
   red blood cells

4. We help your blood to clot.
   platelets

5. We defend your body against infection and disease.
   white blood cells, antibodies

If applying pressure fails to stop the bleeding, call a doctor right away!

Your hardy heart

A continuing heartbeat

Between your lungs, almost in the center of your chest, is your **cardiac muscle,** or heart. This large, hollow muscle is about the size of your fist and weighs only ¼ pound; the heart of an adult weighs about ½ pound. In order to keep your body supplied with nutrients and oxygen, the cardiac muscle contracts around 90 times a minute. It automatically adjusts its speed to the needs of your body—sleep slows it down; excitement and exercise speed it up. Try opening and closing your fist 90 times in one minute. Could you continue to open and close it all day long? Your heart contracts more than 100,000 times each day. During the tiny pause between contractions,

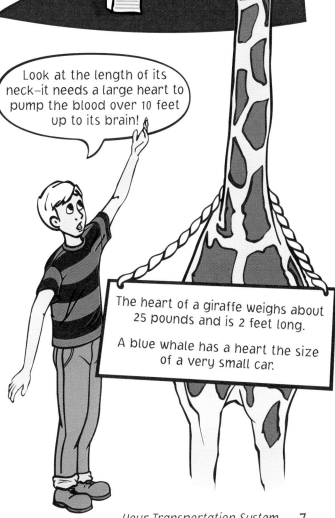

Look at the length of its neck—it needs a large heart to pump the blood over 10 feet up to its brain!

The heart of a giraffe weighs about 25 pounds and is 2 feet long.

A blue whale has a heart the size of a very small car.

your heart rests. Because God designed your heart as an involuntary muscle, you do not need to remember to tell it to contract—the cardiac muscle contracts without your even thinking about it.

Your heart is really two pumps placed side by side that work at the same time. Each pump has two chambers (parts)—the **atrium** [ā′trē·əm], or upper chamber, and the **ventricle** [vĕn′trĭ·kəl], or lower chamber. The upper and lower chambers of the heart contract and relax at different times. A wall of muscle between the two pumps separates the heart into the left side and the right side. Blood enters the heart from large veins, flowing into both the upper chambers, or **atria**, and the ventricles. When the ventricles are almost full, the atria contract, filling the ventricles the rest of the way. After the atria contract, little doorlike flaps called **valves** open, and most of the blood flows down to the ventricles. The atria contract to force any remaining blood into the ventricles; then the valves snap shut to prevent blood from returning to the atria. Immediately the ventricles contract, forc-

ing blood out into the arteries and to your body. Other valves close to keep blood from returning to the ventricles.

The sound of your heart beating—*lub-dub*—is the sound of the valves closing. The valves allowing the blood to flow from the atria down to the ventricles produce the *lub* sound as they snap closed. The *dub* sound is the closing of the valves that let the blood flow out of the ventricles.

The work of the pumps

Each part of the heart was designed for a specific function. When the atria relax, blood flows into them from the veins. The right atrium receives blood containing dissolved carbon dioxide. The right ventricle pumps this blood—which has traveled to all parts of the body—to the lungs to be purified. During the purification process, the carbon dioxide escapes into the lungs. At the same time, since there is little oxygen in this blood, oxygen from the lungs moves into the blood. The left atrium receives the oxygen-rich blood from the lungs, and the left ventricle pumps the oxygen-rich blood through the main artery to the rest of the

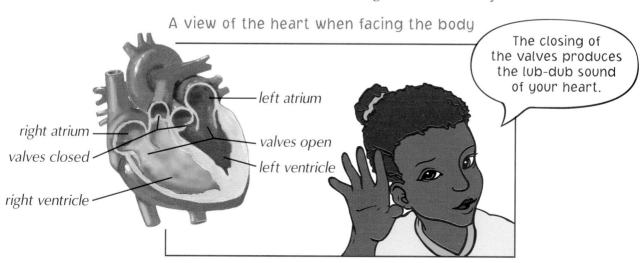

A view of the heart when facing the body

left atrium

right atrium

valves open

valves closed

left ventricle

right ventricle

The closing of the valves produces the lub-dub sound of your heart.

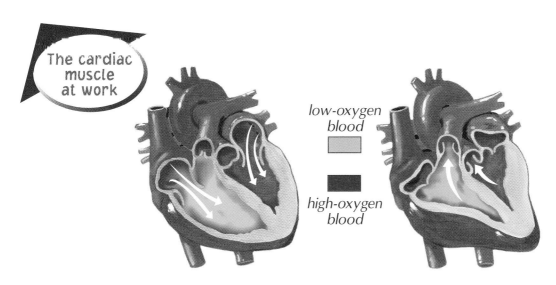

The cardiac muscle at work

low-oxygen blood

high-oxygen blood

body. The left ventricle is slightly larger than the right ventricle, because a larger amount of muscle is needed to pump blood to all parts of the body. The right ventricle sends blood only to the lungs. The blood returns to the right atrium from the veins to complete the cycle again and again.

Although the two pumps of the heart have different jobs, their timing is the same. Because they fill up at the same time, contract at the same time, and relax at the same time, you feel only *one* heartbeat instead of two.

Quick Checkup
Who am I?

1. I am your cardiac muscle.
   heart
2. I am an upper chamber of your heart.
   atrium
3. I am a lower chamber of your heart.
   ventricle
4. We receive blood from the veins.
   atria
5. We pump blood to the arteries.
   ventricles

Pathways through your body

Your blood travels through about 75,000 miles of pipelines to all parts of your body. Remember, your heart actually sends the blood on two different routes—one through your lungs and one through the rest of your body. The right side of your heart receives waste-filled blood from the veins and pumps it to the lungs to be purified. The left side of your heart receives the purified, oxygen-rich blood from your lungs and pumps it out to all parts of your body. The waste-filled blood from your body again enters the right side of the heart.

Because the brain needs a continuous supply of oxygen-rich blood, the blood may make several round trips from the heart to the brain in the amount of time it takes the blood to make one round trip from the heart to a foot and back. Individual blood cells may go to different parts of the body with each trip, but all blood cells follow a specific pathway. This continuous flow of blood around and around the body is called **circulation.**

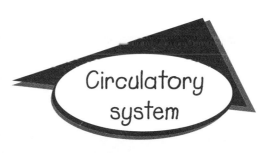

Circulatory system

Follow the path of blood from the right atrium to the right ventricle, the left lung, the left atrium, the left ventricle, and out through the aorta to all parts of the body.

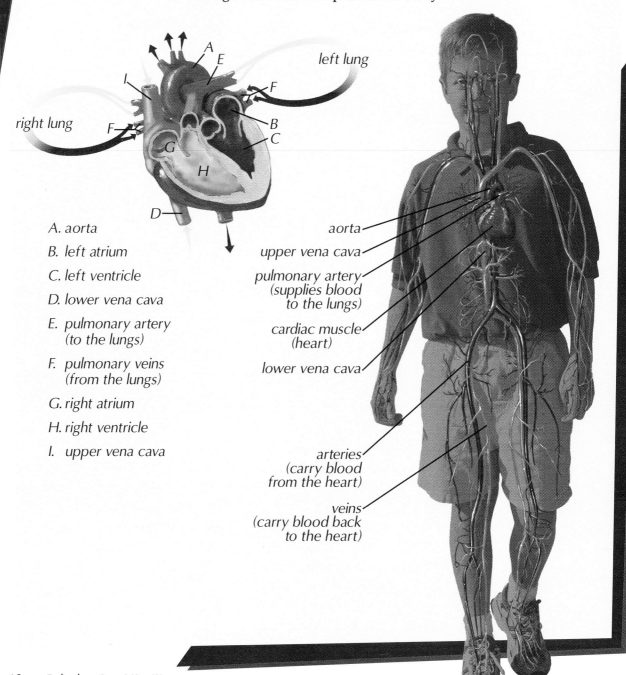

left lung

right lung

A. aorta

B. left atrium

C. left ventricle

D. lower vena cava

E. pulmonary artery
(to the lungs)

F. pulmonary veins
(from the lungs)

G. right atrium

H. right ventricle

I. upper vena cava

aorta

upper vena cava

pulmonary artery
(supplies blood
to the lungs)

cardiac muscle
(heart)

lower vena cava

arteries
(carry blood
from the heart)

veins
(carry blood back
to the heart)

God so designed the **circulatory system**—the heart, blood, arteries, capillaries, and veins—that it takes less than one minute for the blood to flow from your heart, through your body, and back to your heart.

Flowing from the heart

Extending out of the left ventricle of the heart is the largest artery in the body—the **aorta** [ā·ôr′tə]. With each contraction, your heart forces blood into the aorta in a powerful spurt. Immediately after leaving your heart, the blood may travel 12 inches in one second. The arteries expand (stretch) to make room for the blood. When your heart rests between contractions, the arteries spring back to their original size, forcing the blood along. The expanding of the arteries after each heartbeat is called a **pulse.** You can feel the pulse in your body wherever an artery is close to your skin. Can you feel the pulse at your neck? The side of your face? Your wrist? The throbbing you feel is your blood moving through arteries. You should not use your thumb to check your pulse, because your thumb has a pulse of its own.

As the arteries divide and become smaller and smaller, the blood travels less rapidly. The arteries continue to divide until they become microscopic vessels called capillaries, the smallest blood vessels in your body. By the time the blood reaches the millions of tiny capillaries, it is flowing very slowly—the red blood cells pass through a capillary in single file.

Try pressing a finger against the skin on your arm. The area under pressure becomes lighter in color because you keep the blood from flowing through hundreds of tiny capillaries. The walls of the capillaries are so thin that parts of the blood, oxygen, digested food, carbon dioxide, and liquid wastes can seep through them, carrying food and oxygen *to* all parts of your body and removing waste *from* all parts of your body. The walls of the capillaries are not so thin, however, that they leak. They do not allow red blood cells or large proteins, such as antibodies and albumin, to escape through them.

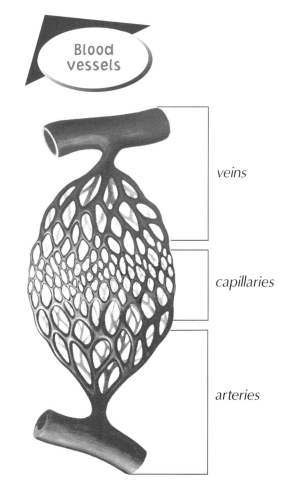

Blood vessels

veins

capillaries

arteries

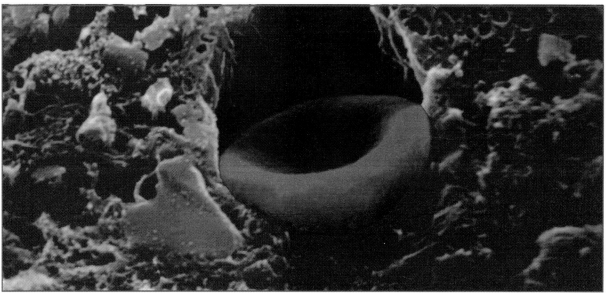

blood cell in a capillary

**Study the circulatory system on page 10
and then label the parts.**

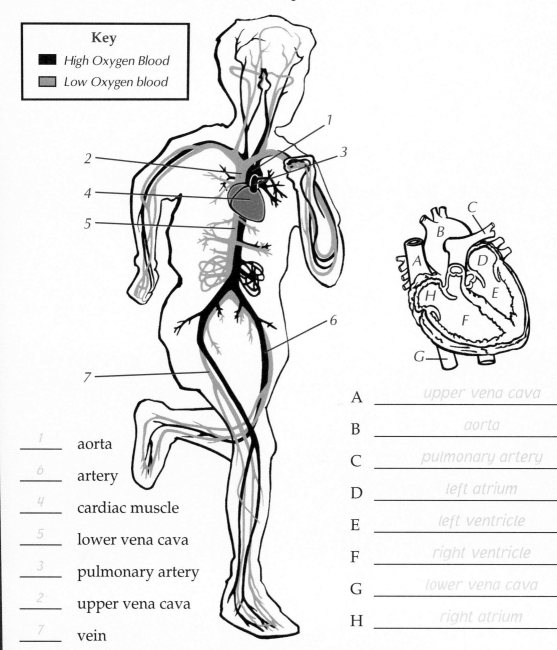

Key

■ *High Oxygen Blood*
▦ *Low Oxygen blood*

_____1_____ aorta

_____6_____ artery

_____4_____ cardiac muscle

_____5_____ lower vena cava

_____3_____ pulmonary artery

_____2_____ upper vena cava

_____7_____ vein

A _____*upper vena cava*_____

B _____*aorta*_____

C _____*pulmonary artery*_____

D _____*left atrium*_____

E _____*left ventricle*_____

F _____*right ventricle*_____

G _____*lower vena cava*_____

H _____*right atrium*_____

Target Heart Rate

Your blood, which carries food and oxygen to your body, circulates better when you exercise regularly. Exercise causes your heart to contract rapidly in order to send extra food and oxygen around your body to different places where they are needed and to carry off waste materials that are formed. Regular, vigorous exercise—**aerobic exercise**—strengthens your heart to pump more blood with each contraction, allowing it to beat less often.

Exercising with too little vigor will not condition your heart. By checking your pulse, or **heart rate,** as you exercise, you can measure how much effort you are putting forth. The rate your pulse must reach and keep for 20 to 30 minutes in order to benefit your heart, lungs, and blood vessels is called your **target heart rate.**

To find out how close you are to your target heart rate, check your pulse immediately after jogging, running, or playing an active game. Do you remember where to feel your pulse? At an artery in your wrist, your neck, or the side of your face. While looking at a second hand on a watch, count the heartbeats you feel in six seconds and

Girls, to determine your target heart rate, subtract your age from 225 and multiply the difference by 75% (.75).

Boys, subtract your age from 220 and multiply the difference by 75%.

walk for thirty seconds. While you run, expand your abdomen when you inhale and flatten it when you exhale. Each day increase your pace (speed) or the distance that you run until you can reach and maintain your target heart rate for 20 to 30 minutes without becoming fatigued (extremely tired).

The best way to condition your whole body is to alternate between different sports or activities, such as running one day, cycling the next, and swimming the day after that. To reach and maintain your target heart rate from cycling, you will need to select gears that do not pedal too easily. When you swim, you may be working harder than your heart rate shows, because the heart contracts more slowly in water. It is also possible to reach aerobic fitness from a very fast walk; however, you will need to increase your time to 35 or 40 minutes five days a week.

Anyone with a weak heart or heart disease should exercise only in the ways recommended by his doctor.

multiply that number by ten. This is your heart rate. If your heart rate after exercising is lower than your target heart rate, you need to work up to your target rate gradually. Exercise should make you perspire, but it should not be painful.

To reach **aerobic fitness,** you can rest as you exercise if you stay active; for example, you may alternate running and walking for 20 or 30 minutes of continuous activity. After your body is warmed up, run for one minute, walk for thirty seconds, run for one minute,

Returning to the heart

The millions of capillaries unite to form veins. After the blood passes through the capillaries, the waste-filled blood flows into very tiny veins and then enters larger and larger veins. Because the blood flowing through the veins is no longer rich with oxygen, its bright red color changes to a darker color. If the veins in the arm can be seen, the color showing through the skin appears to be a bluish color through light-colored skin; the veins may appear darker than the skin color through dark-colored skin.

The blood in your veins is returning to the heart; therefore, it has less pressure than the blood which the heart pumps into the arteries. As you move about, the muscles throughout your body move and squeeze the veins, forcing blood through them. All along the larger veins are valves which prevent the blood from flowing back to the capillaries. The larger veins continue to unite until they are all part of the **venae cavae** [vē′nē kā′vē]—the two large veins which enter the heart. When referring to just one of these two veins, it is called a **vena cava** [vē′nə kā′və]. The upper vena cava carries waste-filled blood from your head and arms to your heart. The lower vena cava carries waste-filled blood from your trunk (the main part of your body) and your legs.

Your blood has a difficult journey from your legs to your heart, because it is fighting gravity. As a person grows older or becomes overweight, the valves in a vein sometimes become weak. Blood then begins to collect in the vein, stretching the wall of the vein and causing pain. These enlarged veins are called **varicose** [văr′ĭ·kōs′] **veins.** By exercising and maintaining proper weight, most conditions of varicose veins can be prevented.

Your blood pressure

The pressure of your blood against the arteries is called **blood pressure.** When your heart is contracting, the pressure is greater than when your heart is relaxing. The pressure of your blood when your heart is contracting is called *systolic* [sĭ·stŏl′ĭk] pressure; the pressure while your heart is resting is *diastolic* [dī′ə·stŏl′ĭk] pressure. The amount of pressure on your arteries depends on how fast your heart contracts, how strong the contractions are, and how much your arteries can stretch. A strong, healthy heart can pump more blood with less effort than a weak heart; thus, a strong heart helps lower blood pressure. Improper diet and insufficient exercise can cause fatty deposits to build up in the arteries, making them less elastic (stretchy).

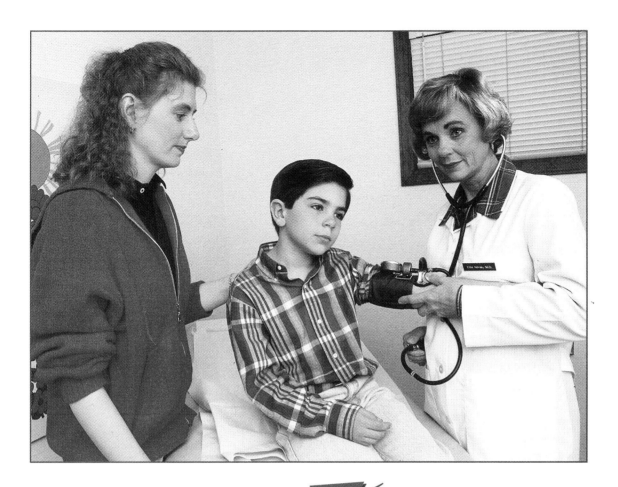

This slows down the flow of blood through the body and increases the work of the heart, which in turn raises the blood pressure. High blood pressure puts extra strain on the heart and the blood vessels.

Remember that it takes less than one minute for the blood to flow from your heart, through your body, and back to your heart. If your heart pumps three quarts of blood through your body every minute, how many quarts of blood would it pump in one day? *4,320 quarts*

to your brain and cause you to feel tired. The time it takes for a tired muscle to become rested depends on how quickly your circulatory system can remove the wastes and replace the food and oxygen; therefore, good circulation of the blood helps prevent fatigue. Because regular, strenuous exercise strengthens your body, you can work and play longer without muscle fatigue if you get sufficient exercise.

Rest gives your body a chance to remove waste materials; it allows your muscles to rebuild worn parts and to restore some of the energy they have used up. You should rest when you begin to feel tired, because tiredness is a sign that your muscles are becoming fatigued. Then you cannot work or play as well as before; you make mistakes because your body and brain are not alert.

Getting restful sleep

The best rest comes from quiet, peaceful sleep. When you are sleeping, your heart rate slows down and less blood is pumped to your voluntary muscles; your breathing also slows down, because your body has less carbon dioxide to rid itself of than when you are active. Your body does most of its resting, growing, and fighting of infections while you sleep. The amount of rest and sleep you need depends on your age, how active you are, and how fast you are growing. For your age, your body needs from nine to

Your body needs rest

Your circulatory system continually transports food and oxygen that every part of your body needs to stay alive. When your muscles work, food and oxygen are used up, and the waste materials—**lactic acid** and **carbon dioxide**—are formed. When wastes are formed faster than they can be removed by the blood, they accumulate (build up) in the muscles. As the blood circulates through your body, some of the wastes are carried

eleven hours of sleep each night. Any time your body is growing rapidly, you need extra sleep. When you are sick, you need more sleep and rest than when you are well. After strenuous work or activity, it is a good idea to go to bed earlier than usual. Because activity helps eliminate waste products, strenuous activity relaxes your body and helps you to get restful sleep.

If you wake up in the morning feeling tired, either you are not getting as much sleep as your body needs or you are not getting restful sleep. You should not eat a meal just before bedtime, since a full stomach may keep you awake or cause you to have nightmares. Vigorous exercise for a long time without sufficient rest can prevent restful sleep or even cause illness. Insufficient rest and sleep may cause you to become grouchy and irritable.

Proper posture as you sleep can also affect your rest. Lying on your side with your knees bent keeps your back straight. You may want to use a small pillow to support your neck.

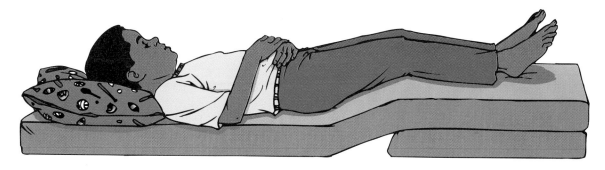

If you sleep on your back, you need your legs raised in order to keep your back flat. You can raise your legs by putting a pillow under your knees or by raising the foot of your mattress.

Try not to sleep on your stomach, because your spine will sag in the middle and your back will not be straight. You should sleep on a firm mattress and wear clean, comfortable night clothes. A lumpy mattress or a pillow that is too thick does not allow your bones to grow straight.

When your body is rested, you are more cheerful, you feel happier, you get along better with others, you feel like being helpful to others, and you feel more like doing your share of the work than when you are tired. Sleep also rests your mind so that you can do good work at school. With proper rest during strenuous activities and with plenty of restful sleep at night, you should wake up each morning feeling refreshed and ready for a new day.

One full day of rest

In addition to the rest you get each day and night, *your body needs one full day of rest every week.* During this time of rest, your body has more time to remove waste materials that build up from hard work and play. God designed our bodies to need a day of rest; He also provided for this day of rest—centuries before scientists discovered that our bodies need it! The Bible teaches, "Six days shalt thou labour, and do all thy work: But the seventh day is the sabbath of the Lord thy God: in it thou shalt not do any work" (Exod. 20:9 and 10). Christians set Sunday aside as a day of rest and worship.

Protecting your heart

Although many people die of heart disease every year, research shows that most of the causes of heart disease can be prevented. You cannot train your heart for emergencies by giving it sudden hard tasks to do; you train it by regular, strenuous exercise. Continual overwork can injure the heart, because it does not allow the heart enough time to get the rest it needs. As a result, the heart becomes weaker rather than stronger. *Both aerobic exercise and sufficient rest will help keep your heart healthy.*

When your body is in good condition, it is easier for it to recover from any illness. Studies also indicate that people who are physically fit may get fewer illnesses than those who are not fit. Whenever you have a cold or other infection, your heart has to work harder to help your body fight the infection. This is one reason you need extra rest when you are sick.

Avoid alcoholic beverages

One thing that some people do that can be very dangerous for the heart is drinking alcoholic beverages, such as beer, wine, and whiskey. Alcohol in one's system can increase the work of the heart, and large amounts of alcohol taken in over a period of time can damage the heart. When a person drinks alcohol, the alcohol does not need to be digested the way foods do. It is absorbed rapidly from the stomach and small intestine and then is carried directly to the liver where it is changed into a toxic (poisonous) substance that destroys liver cells. Whatever alcohol passes through the liver into

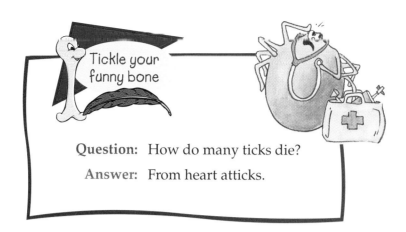
the bloodstream is carried along with the blood to the muscles, the nerves, the brain, the heart—to every part of the body. Alcohol affects the circulation of the blood by causing the blood vessels to expand. When a person drinks much alcohol, the heart pumps less blood with each contraction, causing the pulse, or heart rate, to become very rapid. Continued heavy drinking can weaken the heart and seriously affect its regular work, causing a greater risk of heart disease or a heart attack.

Refuse all forms of tobacco

Smoking cigarettes or using other forms of tobacco is also harmful to the heart; it paralyzes part of the nerve that controls the heart, causing the heart to contract rapidly. Then the heart gets little rest between contractions. Because nicotine (a substance in tobacco) causes the arteries to become narrower, there is less room for the blood to flow through them; and thus the heart has to work even harder, causing high blood pressure. Since this extra work of the heart is not to meet any needs of the body, the heart uses up energy without accomplishing

anything. A person who smokes has a greater risk of getting heart disease and is two or three times more likely to have a heart attack than a nonsmoker. Heavy smoking may cause high blood pressure, rapid heart rate, shortness of breath, and a pain around the heart. The younger a person is when he begins to smoke and the longer a person smokes, the more harm he does to his body.

In addition to the effects of tobacco on the circulatory system, smoking also affects a person's ability in physical

activities. Skill and endurance in sports require a heart that has enough energy to work quickly for a long period of time. Those who injure their bodies with the poisons in tobacco tire more quickly than nonsmokers.

Lower cholesterol buildup

High levels of a certain type of cholesterol [kə·lĕs′tə·rôl]—a fatty substance in the blood—can also harm the heart. Research shows that a diet containing a lot of animal fat raises the level of cholesterol in the blood. Solid fats, eaten in such foods as bacon, sausage, and gravy, increase cholesterol in the blood, whereas liquid fats such as vegetable oils and fish oils do not. Other studies show that fat formed in the body from overeating can also raise the amount of cholesterol in the blood.

Layers of cholesterol build up in the arteries, causing the blood vessels to narrow. This buildup of cholesterol leaves less space through which the blood can flow and may, with time, even choke off the blood supply. Too much cholesterol in the blood is a major cause of heart disease if the person also smokes or is overweight. A proper diet and regular aerobic exercise help clear cholesterol from the arteries.

Become physically fit

A person who is overweight is much more likely to have heart problems than a person who is slim, because the heart of an overweight person works harder.

Since all the fat in the body must receive food and oxygen, the heart must pump blood through more vessels if a person is overweight. Medical research shows that persons with well-conditioned bodies have fewer heart attacks than less active persons, and if they do have attacks, they recover faster. The better condition your body is in now, the longer it will stay in good condition; however, to remain physically fit, it is important for you to continue regular aerobic exercise for the rest of your life.

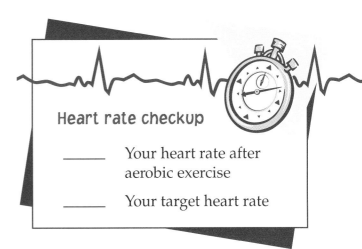

Heart rate checkup

_____ Your heart rate after aerobic exercise

_____ Your target heart rate

Quick Checkup

- ☐ I get regular, strenuous exercise.
- ☐ I rest when I feel tired.
- ☐ I wake up in the morning feeling rested.
- ☐ I refuse to use tobacco, alcohol, and other drugs that are harmful to my body.
- ☐ I am not overweight or underweight.

chapter 1

Comprehension Checkup

I. VOCABULARY: Match the term with the definition.

_A_ 1. the largest artery in the body

_M_ 2. a large vein from the upper or lower body which enters the heart

_L_ 3. a blood vessel which carries blood *to* the heart

_B_ 4. a blood vessel which carries blood *from* the heart

_D_ 5. the smallest of the blood vessels

_I_ 6. the heart rate

_E_ 7. the heart

_F_ 8. the continuous flow of blood around the body

_J_ 9. an upper chamber of the heart

_C_ 10. little doorlike flap

A. aorta

B. artery

C. valve

D. capillary

E. cardiac muscle

F. circulation

G. ventricle

H. plasma

I. pulse

J. atrium

K. varicose vein

L. vein

M. vena cava

II. IDENTIFICATION: Label each part of the heart.

1. _left atrium_

2. _right atrium_

3. _left ventricle_

4. _right ventricle_

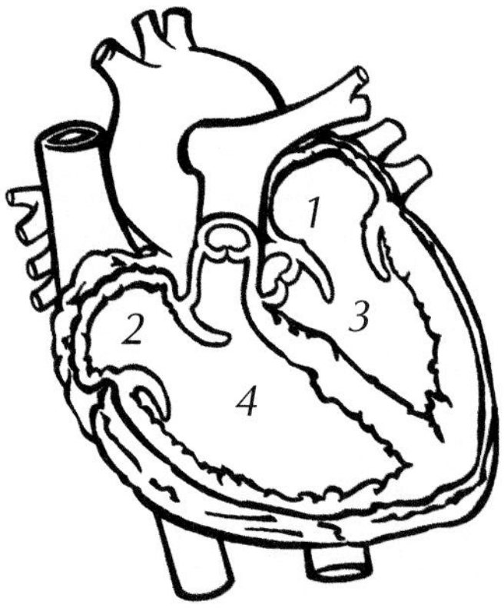

III. COMPLETION: Write the correct answers on the lines.

plasma 1. The liquid part of blood is called __?__ .

bloodstream 2. Food and oxygen are moved from one part of the body to another through the __?__ .

digested food   3. Plasma carries _?_ to every part of the body.

oxygen   4. Red blood cells carry _?_ throughout the body.

infection/disease   5. White blood cells defend the body against _?_ .

clot   6. Platelets help the blood to _?_ .

iron   7. A mineral which helps give red blood cells their color is _?_ .

varicose veins   8. Painful, enlarged veins are known as _?_ .

blood pressure   9. The pressure of your blood against the arteries is called _?_ .

circulatory system   10. The heart, blood, arteries, veins, and capillaries are part of the _?_ .

pulmonary artery   11. The artery that supplies blood to the lungs.

scab   12. A blood clot on your skin is called a _?_ .

IV. EVALUATION

1. Why do alcoholic beverages affect all parts of the body?

   Alcohol is absorbed rapidly by the body and is carried directly to the liver where it is changed into a poisonous substance. The alcohol that passes through the liver is then carried by the bloodstream to every part of the body.

2. How does the use of tobacco affect the various parts of the circulatory system?

   Smoking tobacco causes the heart to contract rapidly and the arteries to become narrower, which may result in high blood pressure, rapid heart rate, shortness of breath, and pain around the heart.

Food for Vitality

Quick! Which foods give you energy? How much fat should you have in your diet? How much protein? Which foods keep you alert in the classroom? Is sugar really harmful? What about cholesterol? Why is too much sodium harmful? What is a balanced diet? It is important to know which nutrients are found in which foods and how often your body needs these nutrients. By continually replacing nutrients that your body uses, you are helping to keep your body healthy.

You know that all foods contain moisture—some contain a great deal, some just a little. The solid (non-moist) part of food is made up mostly of carbohydrates, fats, and proteins. *Carbohydrates* and *fats* supply your body with fuel for energy. If the carbohydrates and fats that you eat are not used for energy, they are stored in your body as fat. *Proteins* provide your body with material for growth and repair. Protein foods also contain some carbohydrates or fats. Meat always has fat with the protein, even if the meat is lean; milk has both carbohydrates and fat with the protein. *Vitamins* and *minerals* are other important nutrients; vitamins, minerals, water, and *fiber* (indigestible carbohydrates) all help your body to function properly.

A balanced diet

A **balanced diet** is a diet that *contains all the nutrients necessary to keep you healthy.* Most foods contain more than one nutrient, but no one food supplies all the nutrients that your body needs. Because some foods are high in certain nutrients and other foods are high in other nutrients, it is important for you to *eat a variety of foods.*

As you read about each nutrient, locate it on the chart on pages 30 and 31 to decide the amount you need and to determine which foods are good sources of the nutrient.

Full of energy

Nutrients are substances found in food that help your body grow and develop; they nourish your body and give you energy. It takes energy to keep your mind alert. It takes energy to play sports. **Energy** is the ability to do work. Your body uses energy for every action—to move, to breathe, to think, to grow, even to stay warm. Repairing body parts when you get hurt takes energy, too. All of this *energy comes from nutrients in the food you eat.*

Carbohydrates

Over half of the food you eat should be in the form of carbohydrates. **Carbohydrate foods,** foods with sugar and starch in them, supply your body with most of its energy. The molecules of carbohydrates are like long chains. Each link in the chain is a simple sugar. The simple sugars link together to form a starch. These chains can be different lengths. Short chains are called *simple carbohydrates;* very long chains are *complex carbohydrates.* Your body changes the starch from these foods into sugar, and then releases the energy stored in the sugar.

Most of the carbohydrate foods you eat should be complex carbohydrates. *Sweet foods such as sugar, jam, syrup, frosting, cake, and candy are not a good source of carbohydrates.* Your body needs vitamins and minerals to change sugar into energy, but refined sugar has no vitamins or minerals in it! The best sources of carbohydrates contain natural sugar or starch as well as vitamins and minerals to change the sugar into energy. When you are not very active, you should get most of the carbohydrates that you need from fruits and vegetables, because they are low in fat.

Carbohydrates

Nutrients Your Body Needs

Nutrients	Good Sources	Functions
Protein	Lean meats, fish, poultry, eggs, milk, buttermilk, powdered milk, yogurt, cheese, soybeans, yeast, wheat germ, legumes • *You need milk and another protein food at each meal.*	• Enables your body to grow • Builds muscles • Fights infection • Repairs your body • Helps your body function properly
Carbohydrates	Fruits, vegetables, whole-grain breads and cereals, brown rice, seeds, nuts, dried beans and peas, honey • *The more active you are, the more you need.*	• Give energy for physical activity • Help heat your body • Allow your body to use protein for growth and repair • Help your body use fats
Fats	Cooking oil, butter, margarine, mayonnaise, cheese, whole milk, egg yolk, nuts, peanut butter, seeds, wheat germ • *You need only a small amount every day.*	• Carry vitamins A, D, E, and K to all parts of your body • Give an extra supply of energy • Help keep your body warm • Help keep your skin from becoming dry and flaky • Keep you from feeling hungry
Fiber	Whole-grain breads and cereals, bran, raw fruits and vegetables, fruits with seeds (figs, berries), nuts • *You need some every day.*	• Helps eliminate waste materials
Liquids	Milk, fruit juice, vegetable juice, water • *You need 6 or more large glasses every day.*	• Help control body temperature • Carry nutrients throughout your body • Help digest food • Help change food into energy • Produce blood, saliva, and digestive juices • Carry wastes from your body

Minerals

Nutrients	Good Sources	Functions
Calcium	Milk, buttermilk, yogurt, ice milk, cheddar cheese, canned salmon and sardines (with bones), shellfish, dark green leafy vegetables (except spinach, chard, and beet greens), broccoli, soybeans, dried dates and figs, barley • *You need milk at every meal.*	• Builds strong bones and teeth • Helps broken bones to mend • Prevents tooth decay • Regulates muscle contractions • Helps you relax
Iodine	Seafood, iodized salt	• Helps your thyroid gland function properly
Iron	Liver, lean meat, shellfish, dark green leafy vegetables, egg yolk, soybeans, dried peas and beans, dried fruits, wheat germ, dark molasses, whole-grain breads and cereals	• Keeps your blood healthy • Helps your body use oxygen • Prevents fatigue
Magnesium	Whole grains, soybeans, dried peas and beans, nuts, dark green leafy vegetables, potatoes, fruits, yeast, molasses • *You need extra whenever you are involved in strenuous or long-endurance activities.*	• Helps change food into energy • Helps your body absorb calcium • Helps your circulatory system work properly • Regulates muscle contractions • Helps you relax

Nutrients	Good Sources	Functions
Phosphorus	Milk, cheese, meat, fish, poultry, eggs, whole-grain breads and cereals, legumes, nuts	• Builds strong bones and teeth • Helps regulate many body functions • Helps store and release energy
Potassium	Fruits, vegetables, soybeans, mushrooms, wheat germ, whole-grain breads and cereals, nuts, yeast, lean meats • *Eat more fruits and vegetables and fewer salty foods.*	• Keeps your heartbeat regular • Helps your nervous system work properly • Helps you think clearly
Zinc	Shellfish, lean meat, poultry, eggs, whole grains, nuts	• Helps repair your body • Heals wounds • Helps your immune system

Vitamins

Nutrients	Good Sources	Functions
Vitamin A	Egg yolk, milk, fish-liver oils, liver, butter, enriched margarine, dark green vegetables, deep yellow fruits and vegetables • *You need to eat at least one dark green vegetable, one deep yellow vegetable, or one deep yellow fruit at two different meals each day.*	• Helps keep your skin healthy and smooth • Helps you see well • Helps the development of bones and tooth enamel • Helps protect against colds and infections
B vitamins	Liver, yeast, wheat germ, brown rice, milk, meat, whole-grain breads and cereals, nuts, most vegetables • *You need some every day.*	• Help your body use protein to build new tissue • Help change food into energy • Help the digestion of your food • Help your body grow at a normal rate • Help keep your blood healthy • Help keep your gums healthy and prevent tooth decay • Help keep the skin around your eyes and mouth smooth and healthy • Help your heart and nervous system work properly
Vitamin C	Citrus fruits, berries, papayas, cantaloupes, tomatoes, broccoli, raw cabbage, Brussels sprouts, green peppers • *You need some every day.*	• Helps your body resist and fight infection • Helps heal cuts, scrapes, burns, and broken bones • Helps keep your gums healthy • Develops strong bones and teeth • Helps prevent allergies • Helps form the material that holds the body cells together • Helps prevent fatigue
Vitamin D	Milk fortified with vitamin D, liver, fish-liver oils, sardines, salmon, tuna, egg yolk	• Helps your body use minerals from other foods to build strong bones and teeth • Helps prevent tooth decay
Vitamin E	Vegetable oils, wheat germ, whole-grain breads and cereals, egg yolk, liver, bean sprouts, cabbage, lettuce, yeast • *The more fats and oils you eat, the more vitamin E you need.*	• Keeps nutrients from being destroyed in your body by oxygen • Helps your body use vitamin A • Increases the amount of vitamin A that can be stored in your liver • Helps change food into energy • Helps keep your heart and skeletal muscles healthy • Helps burns heal faster
Vitamin K	Yogurt, alfalfa sprouts, dark green leafy vegetables, cabbage, cauliflower, egg yolk, liver, soybean oil	• Helps your blood clot properly

Fats and oils

Everyone needs to eat some fats and oils, but most people eat too many. A very small part of your total food intake should consist of fatty foods. Only a little fat is needed to carry the essential fats and fat-soluble (able to be dissolved in fat) vitamins that your body needs.

Fats that are liquid at room temperature are called oils. Oils, such *as vegetable oils* and *fish oils*, are **unsaturated** [ŭn·săch′ə·rā′tĭd] **fats.** *Animal fats,* which are usually solid at room temperature, have to be heated in order to melt; they are mostly **saturated fats.** *Palm oil* and *coconut oil* are also saturated fats. Saturated fats are usually more difficult to digest than unsaturated fats.

Fats and Oils

Products such as margarine and shortening have hydrogen (a gas) added to vegetable oil to make the oil more solid. Many processed foods such as cookies, cakes, crackers, granola bars, and candy bars contain **hydrogenated** [hī′drə·jə·nāt′ĕd] **oil.** The more hydrogen that is added, the harder the oil becomes and the more saturated it becomes.

Medical research shows that large quantities of saturated fat, eaten in such foods as bacon, sausage, hot dogs, and gravy, can contribute to heart disease and cancer; saturated fat also raises the level of cholesterol in the blood. Although your body needs some cholesterol, high levels of a certain kind of cholesterol in your blood are harmful to your heart. Remember that layers of cholesterol gradually build up in the arteries until the arteries become so clogged that the blood has difficulty flowing through them.

If you eat fried foods, fatty meats, sweet rolls, cakes, pies, cookies, and candy bars very often, you are eating too many fats. When you eat fats between meals, you may not feel hungry at mealtime. Then you will not want to eat the nutrients that your body needs.

Protein

When you eat foods containing sufficient carbohydrates and fats, the protein that you eat is spared for growth and repair instead of being used for heat and energy. Because so much of your body is made largely of protein—your skin, nails,

Protein

hair, muscles, internal organs, and even your brain—your body can work well and keep itself repaired only when you eat sufficient protein. Your body needs even more protein to build muscles and to grow; therefore, if you are growing rapidly, you need extra protein. Protein also helps keep your body well; if you are sick, your body needs extra protein to fight the infection and heal itself. Whenever you are involved in strenuous or long-endurance activities, you also need additional protein.

Because your body is so dependent upon protein, you need to eat protein foods every day. Your body can use the protein better when it is divided among three meals, rather than being eaten all at one time. *You need milk and some other protein food at every meal.* Your breakfast should contain protein to sustain your active body throughout the day. While you are in school, protein foods help keep your mind alert so that you can think better. Can you think of something

other than food that helps keep you alert? Getting adequate exercise *and* eating sufficient protein foods will help you do better work at school; you will enjoy school more then, too. Proteins that you eat at your evening meal are used at night while you sleep to repair and build your body cells. You do most of your growing while you are asleep.

Quick Checkup
Name the term.
1. Comes from nutrients in the food you eat
   energy
2. Contains all the nutrients necessary to keep you healthy
   balanced diet
3. Supply your body with most of its energy
   carbohydrates
4. Should be found in less than 1/4 of the food you eat
   fats and oils
5. Makes up much of your body
   proteins

Processed meats, such as sausage, hot dogs, and luncheon meats, are not a good source of protein—they are extremely high in saturated fats.

Vitamins

Other nutrients in foods that keep your body working and growing are vitamins—special helper substances needed in very small amounts. In order to get all the different vitamins that your body needs each day, you must eat a variety of foods. The amount of vitamins in the foods you eat depends on when the foods are harvested, their ripeness, the length of time they are stored, their temperature during storage, and how they are prepared or cooked. Because oxygen destroys many vitamins, most fresh, ripe fruits and vegetables should be stored in tight-fitting containers or plastic bags in the crisper section of the refrigerator—they lose more vitamins if they are stored at room temperature.

Water-soluble vitamins

Vitamin C. Vitamins such as vitamin C and the B vitamins are called water-soluble vitamins because they can be dissolved in water. Vitamin C cannot be stored by your body; therefore, you need to eat foods containing this important vitamin every day. Foods containing the most vitamin C are *citrus fruits*—

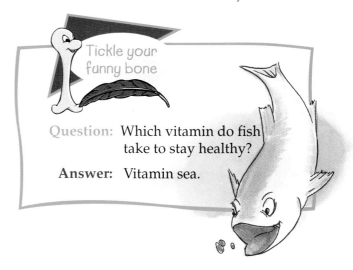

Tickle your funny bone

Question: Which vitamin do fish take to stay healthy?

Answer: Vitamin sea.

oranges, grapefruits, lemons, and limes—and their juices. Refer to the chart of nutrients on pages 30 and 31 for other good sources of vitamin C.

Since vitamin C is easily destroyed, raw fruits and vegetables contain more vitamin C than canned, cooked, or frozen ones. To keep the vitamin C from being destroyed, it is best not to prepare fruits and vegetables until just before you are ready to use them. Vegetables cooked in a microwave oven lose less vitamin C than those prepared by other methods of cooking because the cooking time is shorter and less moisture is needed for cooking.

Vitamin C helps your body make and maintain healthy skin, teeth, and bones. If you have bruises on your arms or legs, this may be a sign that you need more vitamin C.

Vitamin C

Healthful Hint

Ripe fruits and vegetables should be eaten as soon as possible!

The longer they are stored, even in the refrigerator, the more vitamins they lose.

Vitamin B

The B vitamins. There are eight different B vitamins that work together and are needed by every part of your body. Because the B vitamins are not stored well by your body, you need to eat foods every day that contain these vitamins. *Liver* and *wheat germ* are the only foods that contain all of the B vitamins. If your scalp and eyebrows are dry and scaly, if you always feel tired, or if your growth is slow, you may need more B vitamins.

Healthful Hint

Do not eat live yeast that is used in baking!

Uncooked yeast robs your body of vitamins.

Fat-soluble vitamins

The vitamins A, D, E, and K are soluble (can be dissolved) in fat, but not in water. All of these fat-soluble vitamins can be stored in your body.

Vitamin A

Vitamin A. This nutrient, found in foods we get from animals, helps you to see well. In Asia, Africa, and South America, millions of children become blind from a lack of vitamin A. *Dark green vegetables* and *deep yellow fruits and vegetables* contain **carotene** [kăr′ə•tēn], a nutrient that your body changes into vitamin A. Some evidence shows that foods rich in carotene can help prevent cancer.

Vitamin D. This vitamin is frequently called the *sunshine vitamin,* because when sunshine falls directly on your skin, it forms vitamin D in your body. Being outside in the sunshine helps you get vitamin D, but you also need to eat foods that contain it. If you do not get enough vitamin D, it will show in your bone structure. It can cause your front teeth to stick out, your teeth to grow crooked, your chin or forehead to stick out or be

Vitamin D

Vitamin K. Although *yogurt* contains no vitamin K, the bacteria in yogurt helps your body to make this vitamin in the colon (large intestine). *Alfalfa sprouts* and *green leafy vegetables* are excellent sources of vitamin K. When your body does not have enough vitamin K, the blood does not clot properly, causing you to lose too much blood even from a small cut or scratch.

Vitamin K

sunken, and your chest to be narrow and not well developed. A lack of vitamin D can also cause *rickets,* a disease in which the bones soften and may even bend, causing irregular growth and deformities. Because vitamin D is so important for strong, healthy teeth and bones, it is added to milk and some milk products.

Vitamin E. When vitamin E is applied directly to burns and wounds, it can help them heal. A lack of vitamin E can keep your body from using other nutrients that you need. A lack of it also affects both the circulation and the makeup of your blood, causing you to feel tired or weak.

Vitamin E

> ### Quick Checkup
> **Name the vitamin.**
> 1. A water-soluble vitamin that you need daily
>   *vitamin C*
> 2. Eight different vitamins that work together
>   *the B vitamins*
> 3. A fat-soluble vitamin that helps your blood to clot
>   *vitamin K*
> 4. The sunshine vitamin
>   *vitamin D*
> 5. A vitamin that your body can manufacture from carotene
>   *vitamin A*

Minerals

Minerals are nutrients from the soil that are found in many of the foods you eat. The roots of a plant take water and minerals from the soil; then the water and minerals go through the stem to every part of the plant. Your body gets minerals when you eat parts of a plant—fruits, vegetables, seeds, and nuts. You also get minerals from animals that have eaten plants. Important minerals include *calcium, phosphorus, magnesium, potassium, sodium, iron, iodine,* and *zinc.* They are necessary to keep your body growing and functioning well.

Roots taking in water and minerals

Calcium

Calcium

Calcium is the most common mineral found in our bodies. Your blood carries calcium to your bones and teeth to make them grow. *Milk* is the best source of calcium. This includes milk products such as *buttermilk* and *yogurt.* Only hard cheeses such as *cheddar cheese* are high in calcium; however, hard cheeses also contain a lot of fat. **Unless you drink milk with your meals, you probably do not get enough calcium.**

Because nutrients work together to keep you healthy, if even one nutrient is missing from your diet, it affects how your body uses other nutrients. Your body needs vitamin D in order for it to absorb calcium; vitamin C and magnesium help your body absorb calcium, too. When your body does not absorb the calcium that you eat, the calcium does not do your body any good. Calcium and **phosphorus** [fŏs′fər·əs] work together to build strong bones and teeth. Phosphorus, which helps give rigidity (hardness) to your bones and teeth, is abundant in many foods; however, some phosphorus often is not used by the body because of insufficient calcium.

Healthful Hint

Do not discard the water in which vegetables have been cooked.

Add it to soups and stews to add magnesium and other water-soluble nutrients to your diet.

Most of the calcium in your body is in your teeth and bones, but your blood also needs calcium. Your muscles use calcium from your blood to maintain normal muscle tone and strong muscular contractions. Calcium is also necessary for the normal functioning of the nerves. If you do not eat enough foods rich in calcium, or if your body does not absorb the calcium that you do eat, instead of carrying calcium *to* your bones, your blood will take calcium *from* your bones. Therefore, sufficient calcium is extremely important while you are growing. Bones that continually lose calcium may eventually result in **osteoporosis** [ŏs′tē·ō·pə·rō′sĭs], a disease in which the bones of adults become full of holes and thus are fragile and easily fractured. Remember—exercise helps to strengthen your bones, too. Getting sufficient calcium from the foods you eat and exercising regularly can help prevent osteoporosis when you are older.

Rinse tuna fish with tap water for one minute to reduce the amount of sodium.

chart of nutrients on pages 30 and 31 to find which foods are good sources of magnesium. Are all of these foods high in protein, carbohydrates, or fats? Carbohydrates, which digest faster than protein or fats, are a good source for quick energy, too. Do you remember that you also need extra protein for strenuous activities?

Magnesium

Magnesium

Research shows that magnesium, which helps your body to absorb calcium, is also beneficial for regulating the circulatory system and lowering high blood pressure. *Whenever you are involved in strenuous or long-endurance activities, your body needs additional magnesium.* Refer to the

Sodium

Sodium

You usually get all the sodium that your body needs from table *salt*. In fact, *most people eat too much salt.* Foods canned commercially—meats, soups, vegetables—are usually well salted; you also get sodium from *baking soda, baking powder,* and *food preservatives. Pickled foods* and most *processed meats*, such as ham, bacon, sausage, smoked meats, luncheon meats, and hot dogs, also contain large amounts of sodium. Many *packaged foods*, such as crackers, dry soups, and bread are high in sodium, too. If sodium is one of the first ingredients listed on the label, the sodium content is very high. If you eat too much sodium, unnecessary water is stored in your body. Too much sodium also keeps your body from using potassium, which results in muscle weakness, nervousness, mental confusion, irregular heartbeat, and high blood pressure.

Potassium

If you do not eat enough foods rich in potassium, or if your body cannot use the potassium because of too much sodium, you will feel tired and grouchy. You will not be able to think well or do good work at school. A lack of potassium also affects the heart. To keep the amount of potassium and sodium balanced, *eat more fruits and vegetables and fewer salty foods.*

Trace elements

Minerals, such as iron, iodine, copper, manganese, and zinc, that are necessary in very small amounts to keep your body functioning properly are called trace elements.

Iron

Iron is important to your body because it helps build healthy blood. For good sources of iron, refer to the chart of nutrients on page 30. The acids from such foods as buttermilk, yogurt, and citrus fruits and juices help your body to absorb iron. Milk, which is changed into an acid by bacteria in the small intestine, also helps your body absorb iron; therefore, if you drink milk at mealtimes, your body absorbs more of the iron that you eat. Drinking regular tea (or coffee) with your meal or right after a meal prevents your body from absorbing iron. If you do not get enough iron from the food you eat or your body cannot absorb the iron, your body will not be able to make enough red blood cells to keep your blood healthy. Then you will feel weak and tired. When a person has insufficient red blood cells, the condition is known as *anemia* [ə·nē′mē·ə].

Healthful Hint

Eat a tomato slice on your hamburger to more than double the amount of iron your body absorbs.

Iodine

Iodine

If you do not get enough iodine, the thyroid gland (on the front of your neck) cannot do its work properly. This gland affects your growth and health. Insufficient iodine may even cause a *goiter*—a swelling of the thyroid gland that makes the neck look unusually fat.

Iodine has been added to table salt, because in some areas there is no iodine in the soil or water. If you use only *iodized salt*, your body will get the iodine it needs. Salt that has been added to canned or packaged foods may not be iodized salt; that is why some people who eat too much salt still do not get enough iodine.

Zinc

Zinc

A small amount of zinc is necessary for normal growth, for wounds to heal properly, and to keep your body's immune system functioning. White spots on your nails usually indicate a need for more zinc. The best source of zinc is *shellfish*.

Food alone cannot make you healthy; but good eating habits can help keep you healthy and even improve your health. You need to eat enough protein foods for your body to grow and keep itself repaired. You should not eat too many fats and oils, and the ones you do eat should come from sources that contain other nutrients. Over half of the food you eat should be carbohydrate foods—but only enough to supply the energy that your body will use. How is excess energy stored? You need to eat a variety of foods that are good sources of protein, carbohydrates, and fats so that the essential vitamins, minerals, and fiber that your body needs will also be supplied.

Quick Checkup
Name the mineral.

1. The most common mineral found in your body
   calcium

2. A mineral that works with calcium to make your bones and teeth strong
   phosphorus

3. A mineral you need more of when you are involved in strenuous activities
   magnesium

4. A lack of this mineral can cause a goiter
   iodine

5. A mineral that helps keep your blood healthy
   iron

6. A mineral found in table salt
   sodium

Nutrients Your Body Needs

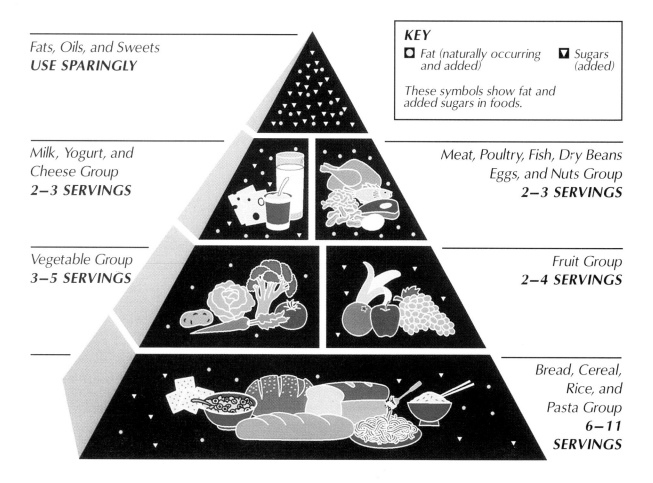

Fats, Oils, and Sweets
USE SPARINGLY

KEY
☐ Fat (naturally occurring and added) ▼ Sugars (added)

These symbols show fat and added sugars in foods.

Milk, Yogurt, and Cheese Group
2–3 SERVINGS

Meat, Poultry, Fish, Dry Beans
Eggs, and Nuts Group
2–3 SERVINGS

Vegetable Group
3–5 SERVINGS

Fruit Group
2–4 SERVINGS

Bread, Cereal, Rice, and Pasta Group
6–11 SERVINGS

Daily food guide

Some people have **malnutrition** (poor nutrition) because they eat only the foods they want to eat. Sometimes poorly nourished people do not know which foods to eat to provide the nutrients their bodies need. If your body is not well nourished, it cannot grow and function properly; therefore, foods containing similar nutrients have been grouped together by nutritionists to help you eat a **balanced diet**—*a diet containing all the nutrients necessary to keep you healthy.*

One such grouping of foods is called the **Food Guide Pyramid.** You do not need something from all of the groups of foods at every meal, but you do need some foods from each group every day. Following a daily food guide allows you to choose a variety of foods as you eat the protein, carbohydrates, fats, vitamins, minerals, and fiber that your body needs each day.

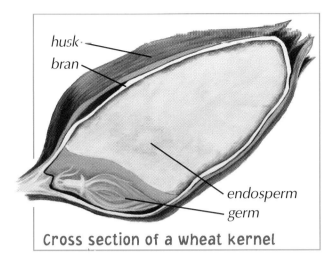

husk
bran
endosperm
germ

Cross section of a wheat kernel

Breads, cereals, rice, and pasta

Breads, cereals, rice, and pasta are good sources of **carbohydrates.** You know that *whole-grain breads* and *cereals* are better for you than white breads or refined cereals. Do you remember why? Whole-grain breads and cereals contain more vitamins, minerals, and fiber.

To make whole-wheat flour, the entire kernel of wheat is ground into flour. To make white flour, only the endosperm, or starchy part is ground into flour. The bran and germ are removed, and some of the vitamins and minerals are not used.

The ingredients that are included in a packaged food are listed on the label. Just because bread is a dark color does not mean that it is whole-grain bread—read the label to find out! *Wheat flour* does not mean whole-wheat flour; it is white flour. Brown sugar and molasses added to bread can make it a darker color.

Breads and cereals containing oat bran are another good source of carbohydrates. Like other brans, oat bran is high in fiber and thus helps keep your digestive system functioning properly.

Your body needs from six to eleven servings from this group each day. The more active you are, the more breads and cereals your body can use.

Fruits

Citrus fruits are one of the richest sources of **vitamin C.** Since your body cannot store vitamin C, you need to *eat foods rich in vitamin C every day.* *Papayas, berries, cantaloupes, tomatoes, broccoli, raw cabbage, Brussels sprouts*, and *green peppers* are not citrus fruits, but they can help supply the vitamin C that your body needs.

Apples, pears, bananas, grapes, watermelons, and plums are just a few of the other fruits that you can enjoy. Most fruits contain fiber. They are also a good source of carbohydrates. **Your body needs from two to four servings of fruit each day.**

Healthful Hint

Most Americans eat less than half the fiber recommended by the National Cancer Institute.

100% RDA

50% RDA

Vegetables

Dark green and deep yellow vegetables are good sources of **carotene** (which your body changes to vitamin A), **vitamins,** and **minerals.** They include such vegetables as *spinach, chard, broccoli, Brussels sprouts, green beans, asparagus, carrots, sweet potatoes,* and *winter squash.* Most vegetables contain **fiber.** They are also a good source of **carbohydrates.** You need to *eat three to five servings of vegetables each day.*

Meats, poultry, fish, dry beans, eggs, and nuts

These foods give your body the protein it needs. Because your body cannot store protein, *you should eat some protein food at every meal.* Your body needs from two to three servings from this group each day. Because many of these foods naturally contain fat, it is good to choose lean meats and to eat more poultry and fish.

Milk, yogurt, and cheese

Milk is the most perfect food that God made. It helps you grow, it helps to keep your body well, and it helps to build strong bones and teeth. It is rich in calcium which is one of the most important minerals for our bodies.

Did you know that you get milk in many foods that you eat? Cheese, yogurt, cottage cheese, ice milk, and pudding are all made with milk. **Your body needs from two to three servings of these dairy products each day.**

Fats, oils, and sweets

Most of the fats and oils in your diet should come from a source that contains other nutrients—such as *cooking oil, butter, whole milk, cheese, egg yolk, seeds,* and *nuts.* **Although you need to eat a small amount of fats and oils, most people eat too many.** Fried foods, bacon and other fatty meats, gravy,

chocolate, coconut, and pastries also contain fats and oils. If you eat these foods often, you are probably eating too many fats and oils.

Good sources of vegetable oils are *safflower oil, sunflower oil,* and *corn oil.* The best margarines to use list liquid oil as the first ingredient. You should avoid fried foods and products made with palm oil or coconut oil since they contain saturated fats.

Healthful Hint

The best margarines to use list liquid oil as the first ingredient.

Quick Checkup

- ☐ I eat 6 to 11 servings from the bread group each day.
- ☐ I eat foods rich in vitamin C every day.
- ☐ I eat at least 3 servings of vegetables daily.
- ☐ I eat some protein foods at every meal.
- ☐ I have 2 to 3 servings of dairy products daily.
- ☐ Most of the fats in my diet come from sources that contain other nutrients.

Energy for activity

Measuring energy

The food you eat provides your body with energy for growth and action. ***The amount of energy that is stored in food*** is measured in **Calories.** Foods that produce a lot of energy are high-Calorie foods; foods producing little energy are low-Calorie foods. Do you remember which nutrients give you energy? Carbohydrates, proteins, and fats.

The number of Calories that you need from the food you eat each day is determined by the amount of energy you use— your size, how fast you are growing, how active you are, and whether you are a boy or a girl. As a general rule, from the ages of nine to twelve, boys require about 200 more Calories a day than girls. If you are growing rapidly or are involved in strenuous activities, your body needs extra Calories. The harder and longer your muscles are used, the more high-Calorie foods you need to provide the extra energy. The season of the year also makes a difference in the amount of energy foods that you need. In cold weather, high-Calorie foods help to keep your body warm. You need fewer high-Calorie foods in hot weather, because less heat needs to be produced inside your body.

Using Calories

People who use the Calories they take in each day are usually neither too fat nor too thin. *The process by which your body produces and uses energy from food* is called **metabolism** [mĭ·tăb′ə·lĭz′əm]. Your rate of metabolism is lowest when you are sleeping or resting. Activity raises your rate of metabolism (how fast your body uses Calories) because you are using up more energy. The faster your rate of metabolism, the more Calories you use.

The following chart lists how many Calories are used for different activities throughout the day. To determine the number of Calories you use in the classroom each day, multiply your weight by the number of Calories used per pound per hour (.8). Multiply this figure by how many hours you spend in the classroom. If you complete an activity in less than an hour, you need to multiply by the fraction of an hour that you spend. For example, if you practice the piano for half an hour, multiply your weight by the number of Calories used per pound per hour (.9); then multiply this figure by .5 to find out how many Calories you used in half an hour. For fifteen minutes, multiply by .25; for forty-five minutes, multiply by .75.

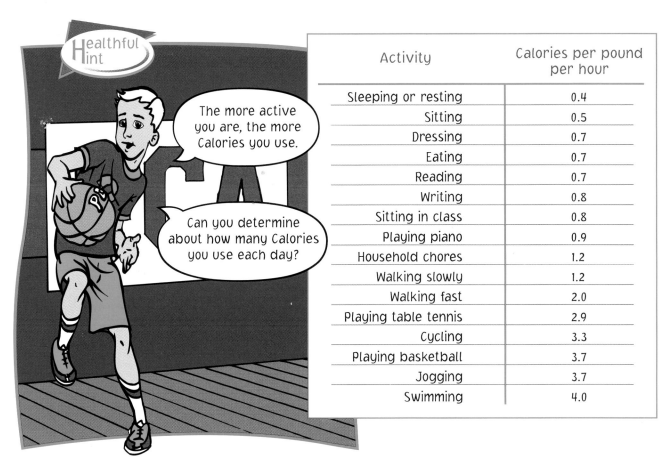

Activity	Calories per pound per hour
Sleeping or resting	0.4
Sitting	0.5
Dressing	0.7
Eating	0.7
Reading	0.7
Writing	0.8
Sitting in class	0.8
Playing piano	0.9
Household chores	1.2
Walking slowly	1.2
Walking fast	2.0
Playing table tennis	2.9
Cycling	3.3
Playing basketball	3.7
Jogging	3.7
Swimming	4.0

By using six teaspoons less fat a day, for the same number of Calories you can eat all of these—

- 1 cup dark green leafy vegetables
- 1/2 tomato
- 1 cup fresh strawberries
- 1 fresh peach
- 1 fresh plum
- 1 oatmeal raisin cookie

A good breakfast

Breakfast is an important meal of the day, because it provides nourishment for your body after a long time without food. What you eat for breakfast determines how well you can work and play all day long. It also affects how you feel and how you act.

Some breakfast cereals are coated with sugar—this much sugar is not good for your body because it is absorbed into the bloodstream too quickly. You should eat cereals that have only a little or no sugar added. A breakfast of complex carbohydrates and protein will last longer into the morning than simple carbohydrate foods.

Try sweetening your cereal with fruit instead of sugar.

Quick Checkup

Name the term.

1. The measurement of the amount of energy in food
   Calorie

2. Foods that produce much energy
   high-Calorie foods

3. Foods that produce little energy
   low-Calorie foods

4. The process by which your body produces and uses energy from food
   metabolism

A good breakfast includes—

- milk
- another protein food, such as an egg, cheese, or meat
- citrus fruit, such as orange juice or grapefruit sections
- a slice of whole-grain toast or a bowl of whole-grain cereal

Check the label on packaged foods to see which ingredients are listed first. If sugar is first on the list, that food has more sugar in it than anything else. You should learn to recognize these other forms of sugar— *honey, molasses, sucrose, glucose, maltose, dextrose, lactose, fructose, corn syrups, corn sweeteners, natural sweeteners, raw sugar,* and *brown sugar.* If two or more kinds of sugar are listed close to the beginning of the list, that product is high in sugar content. If several of them are listed even at the end, it still contains a lot of sugar.

A doughnut, sweet roll, or sugar-coated cereal for breakfast causes your blood sugar to soar. Your pancreas responds by pouring insulin into the blood, and your blood sugar drops lower than it was when you woke up. Then you feel drowsy, you work more slowly, and you cannot concentrate well at school. Scientific research shows that when you eat a nutritious breakfast, you feel alert at school; thus, you can think better and do better work. Even if you are trying to

lose weight, ***never skip breakfast!*** Eating a good breakfast keeps your rate of metabolism higher than if you did not eat.

It is helpful to vary your breakfasts as much as possible. If you get to choose what you want for breakfast, be sure to plan the protein food first. Instead of the usual egg or breakfast meat for protein, try this menu.

- Fruit Cup[1]
- Toasted Cheese Sandwich[2]
- Milk

[1]Cut-up fruit served in orange or grapefruit juice.
[2]Be sure you use whole-grain bread.

Whole-wheat muffins can be substituted for whole-grain toast or cereal. Blueberries, sliced or grated apples, or raisins may be added to the muffins for additional variety.

In place of milk and citrus fruit every morning, try this breakfast drink.

Fruit and Milk Shake

- 3/4 cup milk
- 1/4 cup instant nonfat dry milk
- 1/2 cup fruit-flavored yogurt
- 1 banana, cut and frozen
- 1/2 cup orange juice, chilled

Put all of the ingredients in a blender; cover and blend until smooth. Makes two large servings.

Get up early enough that you can have a pleasant breakfast without being rushed.

A good lunch

Do you eat only those foods that you like? The right kind of lunch will give you more energy to think clearly, to work hard, and to play.

Remember that you need complex carbohydrates and protein for lunch to help keep you alert. What other protein foods may be eaten instead of meat? A fruit or vegetable salad may take the place of the raw fruit or vegetable. A simple dessert, such as fruit-flavored yogurt, pudding, fruit, or peanut butter cookies may be added. For a tasty dessert, spread peanut butter between two oatmeal cookies to make a peanut-butter cookie sandwich.

Soup and a simple dessert, such as fruit, peanut butter cookies, or oatmeal raisin cookies, may be added. If you drink iced tea or a soft drink instead of milk, your body does not get the nourishment it needs. If you eat much candy or potato chips, you will not be hungry for the food your body needs.

Healthful Hint

A good lunch includes—

- milk
- another protein food, such as meat, a meat sandwich, or a meat casserole
- one or more vegetables
- a crisp raw fruit or vegetable

FUEL
4
FITNESS

Record the foods you eat at lunch for one week. Some foods may go under more than one heading. Be sure to record if the fruits and vegetables are cooked or raw.

	Protein	Carbohydrates	Fats	Vitamins	Minerals
Monday					
Tuesday					
Wednesday					
Thursday					
Friday					

Did you eat a protein food every day? Did you get calcium every day? Did you eat a raw fruit or vegetable each day? Did you eat too many fats? Too many sweets?

Healthful Hint

If you bring a lunch box to school, make sure you pack—

- milk
- another protein food such as meat, egg, cheese, or peanut butter sandwich on whole-grain bread
- a crisp raw fruit or vegetable

Healthful Hint

Your lettuce will stay fresh and crisp, and your sandwich won't be soggy.

Pack lettuce and tomato slices in separate sandwich bags; add them to your sandwich when you are ready to eat.

Healthful Hint

A good dinner includes—

- milk
- another protein food, such as meat, poultry, or fish
- one or more cooked vegetables
- a fruit or vegetable salad

A good dinner

Dinner time should be one of the most pleasant times of the day. It is a meal that everyone in the family usually tries to eat together. You should not eat a large evening meal, because your body needs most of its nutrients earlier in the day. A large meal also takes longer to digest than a small one. If your body does not have time to digest the food before you go to bed, you will not sleep well.

Soup, whole-grain bread or rolls, and a simple dessert may be added. Eating soup at the beginning of a meal starts your digestive juices flowing. This helps your body digest the rest of the food you eat. Soups also keep you from eating too much food when you are very hungry because they give you a feeling of fullness.

Preparing good snacks

If you eat between meals, you should eat foods that give you more nutrients. A good snack will keep up your energy so that you will not be hungry again in just a short while. Some good snack foods are *fresh fruits, raw vegetables, hard-cooked eggs, cheese, crackers with peanut butter or cheese, small meat or egg sandwiches* (made with whole-grain bread), *yogurt, nuts, soybeans, sunflower or pumpkin seeds,* and *whole-grain cereals.* For variety, you may want to combine snack foods.

Drink a glass of *milk, fruit juice,* or *vegetable juice* with your snack instead of a soft drink. Milk and fruits can also be combined for a refreshing drink.

Fruit Cooler

- 1 cup milk
- 1 banana, cut and frozen
- 1 cup berries or pineapple

Put all of the ingredients in a blender; cover and blend until smooth. Makes two servings.

Many soft drinks contain caffeine and sugar. Remember—*sugar and most sweet foods do not have other nutrients that your body needs.* If you snack on sweet foods, you probably will not get enough protein, vitamins, and minerals. When you do eat sweet foods, eat them at the end of a meal—do not eat them for a snack. Learning what foods *not* to eat is as important for good nutrition as knowing which foods are good for health. Become a sugar detective—check the labels! It may surprise you to learn that the ketchup you put on your hamburger contains more sugar than ice cream.

Tickle your funny bone

Question: What is a pig's favorite snack food?

Answer: Spighetti.

Quick Checkup

- ☐ I never skip breakfast.
- ☐ I save my dessert until the end of my lunch.
- ☐ I eat a variety of foods for dinner.
- ☐ I do not regularly eat sweet foods between meals.

Energy input/output balance

Maintaining your proper weight

Your weight is determined by the amount of energy you take in through food and the amount of energy your body uses. You need only the number of Calories from food that your body uses each day. Taking in more Calories than you use results in added weight; too few Calories can cause loss of weight.

By watching your weight, you can tell about how many Calories your body needs to keep you healthy and full of energy. If you have plenty of energy throughout the day, you are probably taking in and using about the right

number of Calories. If you are thin and feel weak or tired, you may not be getting sufficient Calories. If you are overweight, you probably are not getting enough exercise, and you may be eating too many high-Calorie foods.

Be sure that if you eat fewer Calories, you do not eliminate necessary nutrients. Everyone needs the same nutrients, but not the same amount of nutrients. Protein foods that stay in your stomach for a longer time than sweet foods (simple carbohydrates) keep you from feeling hungry longer. Foods that are high in fiber are bulky—they take up a lot of room in your stomach; therefore, they satisfy your hunger with fewer Calories.

Poorly chosen snack foods can have a big effect on your weight. Potato chips, a doughnut, a candy bar, or a sugar-sweetened drink would be over one hundred Calories.

This weight gain is not noticed by the day or week (less than $\frac{1}{4}$ pound each week). But if you gain ten extra pounds above your ideal weight each year, how many extra pounds will you weigh by the time you are twenty years old?

Obesity is harmful

Excessive weight interferes with your play and work. It makes it more difficult to move quickly and skillfully in active games. It causes fatigue. An overweight person's back and feet may hurt because they have extra weight to support. Being overweight may also cause poor digestion and can harm your liver, kidneys, and heart. Since all the fat in the body must receive food and oxygen, the heart must work harder to pump blood through more vessels if a person is overweight. Fat that is formed in the body from overeating can also raise the

Food for Vitality 53

Six hundred Calories eaten in a few moments from pie with ice cream could be traded for more than 15 pieces of raw vegetables and fruit.

That's a lot of food to be munched on throughout the day.

amount of cholesterol in the blood. Too much blood cholesterol is especially harmful if a person smokes cigarettes or is overweight.

If you need to lose weight, you should exercise more and eat fewer sweet foods and fatty foods that are high in Calories but do not provide the nutrients that your body needs. In place of these high-Calorie foods, you should eat more fruits and vegetables.

Regular exercise, along with the right kinds and amounts of food, will help you control your weight. You may have heard that the best exercise for losing weight is "pushing away from the table." Do not forget that you are still growing, and unless you are overweight now, you should gradually be gaining pounds. If you are seriously overweight or under-weight, you should see a doctor.

Heart rate checkup

_____ Your heart rate after aerobic exercise

_____ Your target heart rate

Tickle your funny bone

Question: What does a 200-pound parrot say?

Answer: Polly wants a cracker NOW!

Question: After a strenuous workout, how does a fish check its weight?

Answer: It uses its scales.

Good habits for top-notch nutrition

- Eat a variety of foods.
- Eat some protein food at every meal.
- Have two to three servings of dairy products each day.
- Eat foods rich in vitamin C every day.
- Eat at least two servings of fruit and three servings of vegetables each day.
- Eat more fruits and vegetables and fewer salty foods.
- Avoid too many sweet foods.
- Avoid too much saturated fat.
- Avoid harmful beverages.
- Maintain your proper weight.

Raising your rate of metabolism

You know that stretching and warm-up exercises reduce strain on your body. They also allow more blood to flow to your muscles, which increases your rate of metabolism. Besides using more energy, exercise helps to speed up your rate of metabolism for hours *after* you exercise. Thus, early morning exercise helps you to mentally and physically accomplish more during the day.

Swimming is good aerobic exercise for someone who is overweight, because the heart does not have to pump as hard as it does for exercise in an upright position. In addition to helping you lose weight, aerobic exercise actually fights diseases caused by being overweight—high blood pressure, diabetes, high cholesterol—as it strengthens the heart. Medical research shows that persons with well-conditioned bodies have fewer heart attacks than less active persons, and if they do have heart attacks, they recover faster.

Quick Checkup

True/False

1. Everyone needs the same nutrients.
   true
2. Everyone needs the same amount of nutrients.
   false
3. Exercise reduces your rate of metabolism.
   false
4. Fat that forms from overeating raises the blood cholesterol.
   true
5. Obesity harms the heart.
   true

Dodge Ball Run

Exercising your large skeletal muscles helps to break down excess fat and improve your muscle tone. Dodge Ball Run, which may be played by either a large or a small group, needs a **playing field** about 30 feet wide and 60 feet long. If more than 20 are playing, the field may need to be wider than 30 feet. The **line marking home base** should be clearly marked. A **base** that is used in baseball can be used to mark the away base. Additional equipment includes **two soccer balls** or large rubber balls.

30 feet

home baseline

away base

60 feet

Divide into two equal teams, with one team lining up behind the home base line and the other team standing out in the playing field. As soon as the two soccer balls are rolled from the away base onto the field, three runners behind the home base line begin to run toward the away base. They may dodge and run in any direction as they try to run to the away base and back across the home base line without being hit by the ball. Three runners must always be on the playing field; however, the runners do not need to stay together. When a runner is hit with the ball, he must raise his hand, and the next runner begins to run. A runner that has been hit by the ball must return to the home base line without hindering the fielders. When a runner touches the away base and crosses the home base line without being hit by the ball, he scores two points for his team, and the next runner begins to run.

The fielders try to throw the ball and hit the runners before they return to the home base line. The fielders may run after the ball, but once a fielder is holding the ball, he cannot walk or run. The fielder may throw the ball at a runner, or he may throw the ball to another fielder. A foul is called if a fielder carries the ball, if a fielder blocks or holds a runner, if a runner fails to touch the away base, or if a runner fails to raise his hand and return immediately to the home base line after he is hit by the ball.

Each successful run scores two points, and each foul against a player scores one point for the opposing team. Each team should have the same number of times to be the runners so that the team having the most points at the end of the game is the winner.

If your group is small, use only one ball and have just two runners on the field at a time.

Comprehension Checkup

I. VOCABULARY: Match the nutrient with its function or description.

_____I_____ 1. provide your body with material for growth and repair

_____C_____ 2. foods containing sugar and starch

_____D_____ 3. should only be a very small part of the food you eat

_____L_____ 4. a water-soluble vitamin that you need daily

_____A_____ 5. eight different vitamins that work together

_____K_____ 6. a vitamin your body can manufacture from carotene; helps your eyesight

_____M_____ 7. the sunshine vitamin

_____N_____ 8. a fat-soluble vitamin that helps your blood to clot

_____B_____ 9. the most common mineral found in your body

_____H_____ 10. a mineral that works with calcium to make your bones and teeth strong

_____G_____ 11. a mineral you need more of when you are involved in strenuous activities

_____J_____ 12. a mineral found in (not added to) table salt

_____F_____ 13. a mineral that keeps your blood healthy

_____E_____ 14. a lack of this mineral can cause a goiter

A. B vitamins
B. calcium
C. carbohydrates
D. fats and oils
E. iodine
F. iron
G. magnesium
H. phosphorus
I. proteins
J. sodium
K. vitamin A
L. vitamin C
M. vitamin D
N. vitamin K

II. COMPLETION: Write the correct answers on the lines.

_____milk_____ 1. The best source of calcium is _?_ .

_____energy_____ 2. The ability to do work is called _?_ .

minerals   3. Nutrients from the soil that are found in many foods you eat are ? .

nutrients   4. Substances found in food that help your body grow and develop are called ? .

malnutrition   5. Another name for poor nutrition is ? .

balanced diet   6. A diet containing all the nutrients necessary to keep you healthy is a ? .

Calorie   7. The measurement of the amount of energy in food is called a ? .

metabolism   8. The process by which your body produces and uses energy from food is called ? .

III. TRUE/FALSE

true   1. Osteoporosis is a disease in which the bones of adults become fragile.

true   2. A goiter is a swelling in the neck that is caused by insufficient iodine.

false   3. Rickets is a condition in which a person has too few red blood cells.

false   4. Anemia is a disease caused by a lack of vitamin D.

IV. EVALUATION

1. Which would produce the greater number of Calories—a pound of lean meat or a pound of butter? Why?

   A pound of butter; butter contains more fat.

2. Why is it important to eat a variety of foods?

   No one food contains all the nutrients your body needs.

Your 30-foot-long Canal

The beginning of the 30-foot-long tube through your body is your mouth. Along this tube, or canal—the **alimentary** [ăl′ə·měn′tə·rē] **canal**—the food you eat is broken down into smaller parts and changed into a thick liquid. Before any food can be used by your body, the food must be changed into a liquid form. *The breaking down of food into a form that can be used by the body* is called **digestion**. The parts of the **digestive system** along the alimentary canal include the *mouth*, where the food is chewed and mixed with saliva; the *esophagus* [ĭ·sŏf′ə·gəs], a tube which carries food from the mouth to the stomach; the *stomach*, where food is churned and mixed with digestive juices; the *small intestine*, where food is absorbed by the blood; and the *colon* [kōl′ən], which carries the waste parts of the food from the body.

Digestive
system

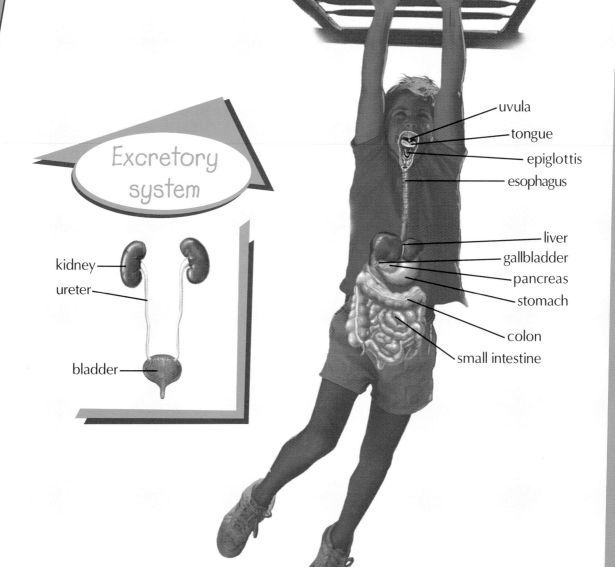

Excretory
system

kidney

ureter

bladder

uvula

tongue

epiglottis

esophagus

liver

gallbladder

pancreas

stomach

colon

small intestine

Digestion begins

As soon as food enters your mouth, it begins a long, slow trip through your alimentary canal. Using the diagram on page 62, follow the route food takes as it is being digested.

The food is broken into small pieces by chewing. Your teeth have different jobs—each kind is necessary to chew your food well. Your front teeth, or **incisors** [ĭn·sī′zərz], bite and cut your food. The teeth next to the incisors are called **cuspids** [kŭs′pĭdz], because they have one cusp, or point. These teeth tear apart coarse fruits, vegetables, and meats. Next to the cuspids are primary molars or **bicuspids** [bī·kŭs′pĭdz]. Sometime between the ages of nine and eleven, bicuspids grow in to replace the primary molars. Bicuspids, which have two points or cusps, tear and crush the food. In the back part of your mouth are the **molars,** which grind your food into tiny pieces. The last molar on each side of the jaw is called a **wisdom tooth.** Your wisdom teeth will probably grow in when you are between 17 and 25 years old.

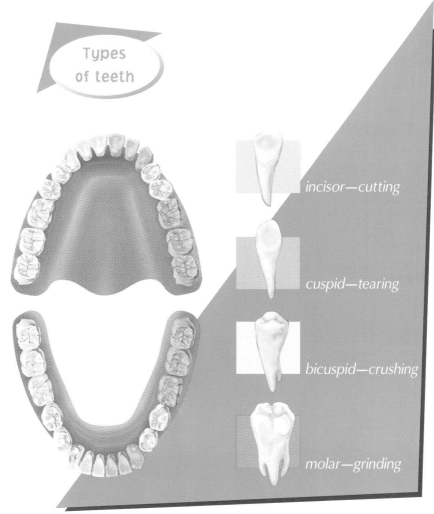

Types of teeth

incisor—cutting

cuspid—tearing

bicuspid—crushing

molar—grinding

Chewing is important

Every mouthful of food should be chewed thoroughly to break the food into fine bits—dry foods require longer chewing than soft, creamy foods. Other changes are also taking place while you chew. The food is mixed with a digestive juice, a colorless liquid called **saliva,** that flows into your mouth. As you chew your food, saliva pours from the six **salivary** [săl′ə·vĕr′ē] **glands** in your upper and lower jaws and under your tongue. Before food is even swallowed, saliva begins the digestion of carbohydrates, contained in foods such as bread or potatoes, by changing the complex starch into sugars that can be dissolved.

The mixing of saliva with the food increases the taste of the food, and the pleasing taste makes the gastric juice in the stomach begin to flow. Thus, the more food is chewed, the easier it is to digest, because it is crushed into tiny pieces and there is more digestive juice to work on it. You should always be sure to swallow the food in your mouth before you take a drink. Do you know why? If

Your teeth must be hard in order to cut, tear apart, crush, and grind food. If you eat a well-balanced diet, your teeth will get the calcium, phosphorus, and vitamins they need to grow strong and healthy. Do you brush your teeth after every meal? Do you clean between your teeth with dental floss or tape? Because the work of your teeth is so important for proper digestion, it is essential that you care for them.

Tickle your funny bone

Question: What bird is at every meal?
Answer: A swallow.

Question: What happens if a tick eats too fast?
Answer: It gets tickups.

you take a drink while food is in your mouth, you will probably wash down food that is not thoroughly chewed.

Through the esophagus

Your tongue helps mix the food with saliva as you chew. Just before you swallow, your tongue forms the chewed food into a ball and pushes it to your **pharynx** [făr′ĭngks: throat]. At the same time that you swallow, your **epiglottis** [ĕp′ĭ·glŏt′ĭs], a tiny flap of cartilage, closes the opening to your **trachea** [trā′kē·ə: windpipe] so that food cannot block the flow of air into your lungs. From your pharynx, the softened food passes through a long tube called your **esophagus.** The contracting of muscles in the esophagus forces food through the canal to your stomach in just four or five seconds. Water can travel through your esophagus in even less time. Because of the muscular action, food moves through your esophagus to your stomach even if you are standing on your head!

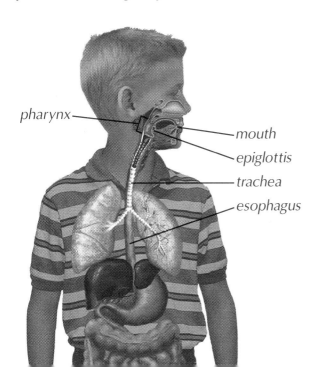

pharynx
mouth
epiglottis
trachea
esophagus

A storage tank

Your food is churned

Your **stomach** is a small elastic bag made of bands of muscles that stretch as food enters it from the esophagus. The *major purpose of the stomach is to store food* and release it a little at a time into the small intestine for further digestion. Another purpose of the stomach is to begin protein digestion. In the stomach's lining are thousands of tiny glands filled with **gastric juice**— a digestive juice which softens foods, kills bacteria, and starts digesting protein foods such as meat, eggs, and milk. Water, vitamins, and minerals do not need to be digested. Water is absorbed into the bloodstream without any

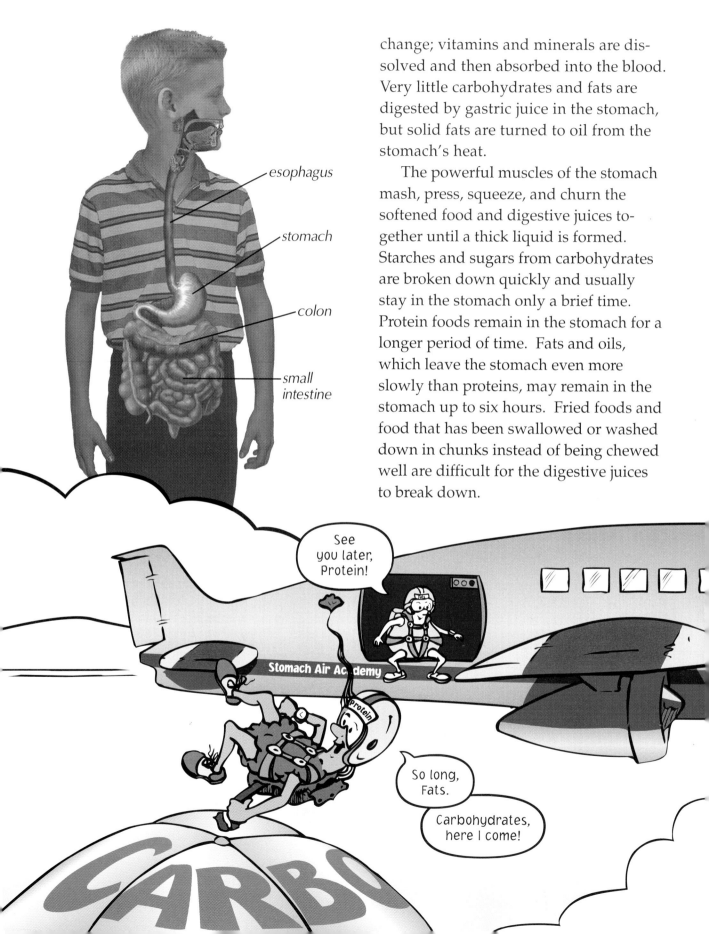

change; vitamins and minerals are dissolved and then absorbed into the blood. Very little carbohydrates and fats are digested by gastric juice in the stomach, but solid fats are turned to oil from the stomach's heat.

The powerful muscles of the stomach mash, press, squeeze, and churn the softened food and digestive juices together until a thick liquid is formed. Starches and sugars from carbohydrates are broken down quickly and usually stay in the stomach only a brief time. Protein foods remain in the stomach for a longer period of time. Fats and oils, which leave the stomach even more slowly than proteins, may remain in the stomach up to six hours. Fried foods and food that has been swallowed or washed down in chunks instead of being chewed well are difficult for the digestive juices to break down.

esophagus

stomach

colon

small intestine

The stomach at work

In 1822 at an army post in northern Michigan, Dr. William Beaumont, a young army surgeon, was called upon to care for an 18-year-old who had been struck by an accidental shotgun blast. The shot, which went through Alexis St. Martin's left side, tore a gaping hole in his stomach. With Dr. Beaumont's care, St. Martin recovered, but the hole in his stomach never completely closed. A flap of loose skin came down over the hole, and Dr. Beaumont could lift up this flap and watch the stomach at work.

From observing St. Martin's stomach, Dr. Beaumont learned that the stomach finishes its work more quickly with some foods than with others. Do you remember which foods stay in the stomach the longest? Which foods leave the stomach first? Dr. Beaumont noted the importance of saliva and the work of the teeth in digestion. He also learned that food digests better when meals are eaten regularly and when the stomach has a chance to rest between meals. Whenever St. Martin was unhappy or worried, the digestive juice in his stomach did not flow as freely as usual, and with less gastric juice, the stomach could not do its work as well as it should. However, when St. Martin was happy, gastric juice poured out to mix with the food. Another thing Dr. Beaumont observed was that alcoholic drinks made the stomach red and sore-looking. Again, the stomach did not work as well as it should.

Healthful Hint

Keep your mealtimes happy.

Quick Checkup

True/False

1. The major purpose of the stomach is to store food.
   true

2. Saliva is a digestive juice in the stomach.
   false

3. Fats are changed to oil in the stomach.
   true

4. Carbohydrates remain in the stomach longer than protein foods, fats, and oils.
   false

5. Alcoholic drinks harm the stomach.
   true

Digestion continues

As the food becomes soft enough, your stomach squeezes out the thick liquid with small, continuous squirts. This continues until all of the food in your stomach is squeezed into the **small intestine**—a 20-foot-long tube of muscle and other tissues that is coiled up just below the stomach.

As the partly digested food moves into your small intestine, intestinal juice flows from millions of tiny glands in the walls of the small intestine. Other digestive juices, which are made or stored in your *pancreas* [păng′krē·əs], your *liver*, and your *gallbladder* [gôl′blăd′ər], pour through **ducts,** or tubes, into your small intestine. These digestive juices complete the digestion of carbohydrates and proteins that was started in your mouth and stomach. They also digest the fats and oils. *Most of the food you eat is digested (changed so that it can dissolve in water) in your small intestine.*

Most carotene, the substance found in deep yellow and dark green vegetables, is changed to vitamin A in your intestinal wall.

Another important function of your small intestine is to move water, vitamins, minerals, and the digested food into your bloodstream, where it is transported to all parts of your body. This process by which food is made available to your body is called **absorption.** The cells in your small intestine that do the absorbing use more oxygen and give off more carbon dioxide when they do the work of absorbing than while they are not absorbing. Thus, the process of absorption uses energy.

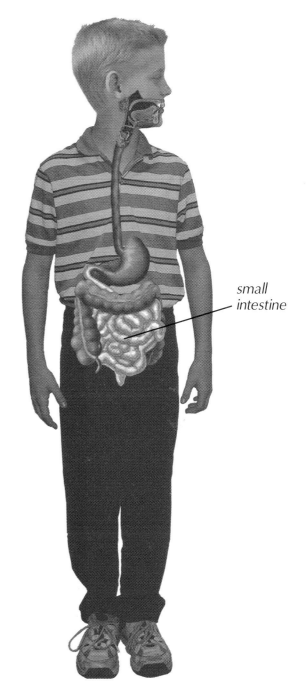

small intestine

Study the digestive system on page 62 and then label the parts.

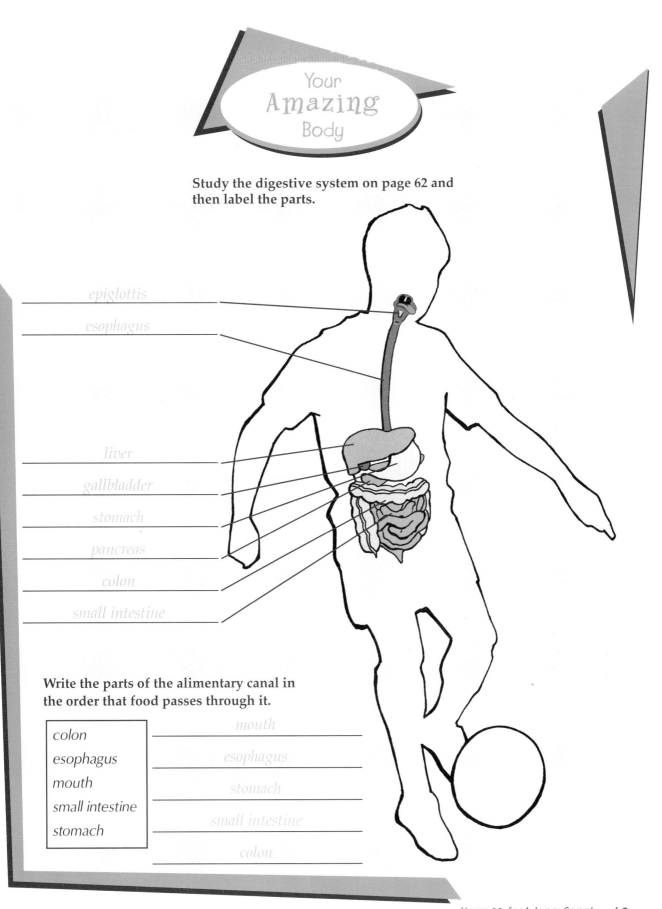

epiglottis

esophagus

liver

gallbladder

stomach

pancreas

colon

small intestine

Write the parts of the alimentary canal in the order that food passes through it.

| colon |
| esophagus |
| mouth |
| small intestine |
| stomach |

mouth

esophagus

stomach

small intestine

colon

An important manufacturing plant

Your **liver**—the largest organ inside your body—is located just below the diaphragm in the upper right portion of your abdominal cavity. It is partially surrounded by your ribs and is connected to your alimentary canal by a tube. Every second, millions of red blood cells finish their work in your body and die. Your liver filters out these dead cells, recycles the iron from them, and sends it to your long bones, where it is used as part of new red blood cells.

Your liver uses another part of the dead red blood cells to make **bile,** a greenish-colored digestive juice that is mixed with food in your small intestine. Bile salts, important substances contained in bile, are made with cholesterol which is manufactured in your liver. Bile salts help in the digestion of fats and oils and are necessary for the absorption of vitamin E. Oil cannot be digested in your

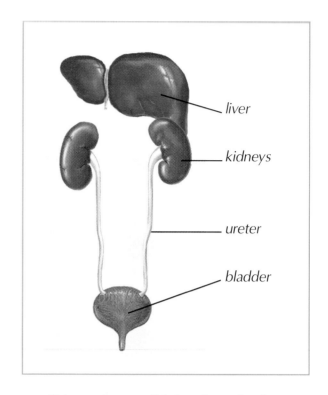

liver

kidneys

ureter

bladder

small intestine until it has been broken into tiny droplets and spread evenly through the digestive juices. Bile keeps the oil droplets separated and mixed with the digestive juices so that the oil can be digested. Each day, your liver produces about one quart of bile and stores it in your **gallbladder.** Besides helping to digest and absorb fats and oils, bile carries some waste material out of your body.

The blood from the small intestine, with its rich supply of digested food, passes through your liver before being pumped throughout your body. Your liver stores minerals and the vitamins A, B-complex, D, E, and K until your body needs them. Another function of your liver is to change some of the carotene found in deep yellow and dark green vegetables into vitamin A.

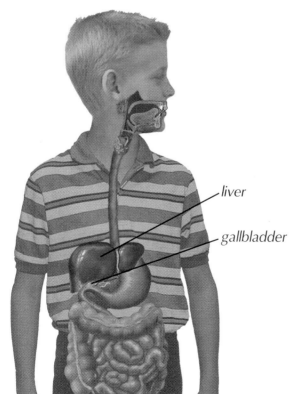

liver

gallbladder

All of the blood from your stomach and intestines passes through your liver before it gets to your heart. A large amount of this blood contains wastes which have been collected throughout your body. Another duty of your liver is to help remove these wastes. After digestion breaks down proteins in the food, your liver forms urea from the parts and sends the urea, which contains waste, to your **kidneys,** bean-shaped organs about the size of your fist. The kidneys reabsorb water and other useful materials back into the blood, and the filtered wastes drain into a muscular pouch, called the **bladder,** to be removed from the body in the urine.

The liver also helps remove poisons that have formed in the small intestine during digestion. Filtering too much poison from the blood can poison the liver. A poisonous chemical which is produced when alcohol is broken down

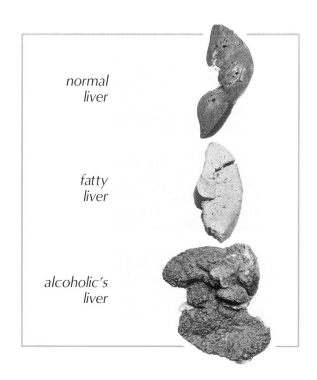

normal liver

fatty liver

alcoholic's liver

is extremely harmful to the liver. With heavy drinking of alcoholic beverages, a condition called *fatty liver* develops. If the person continues to drink alcoholic beverages, the liver cells swell and die, resulting in *cirrhosis* [sĭ·rō′sĭs: a gradual deterioration] of the liver. When enough scar tissue replaces the healthy liver cells, the liver can no longer function, causing death.

During digestion, more sugar is absorbed in your small intestine than the body can use at that time for heat and energy. The blood from the small intestine—containing sugar from the digested food—passes through your liver before it is pumped all around your body by your heart. Because too much sugar in your blood is dangerous to your health, God designed the liver to remove the extra sugar from the blood and store it until the body needs it.

Healthful Hint

Never drink alcoholic beverages!

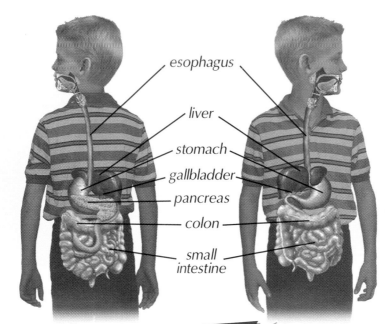

esophagus
liver
stomach
gallbladder
pancreas
colon
small intestine

Keeping your sugar level safe

When you eat too many simple carbohydrates, the amount of sugar in your blood becomes high. Your **pancreas,** which is located between your stomach and your small intestine, makes a substance called **insulin** that helps your liver store the excess sugar. If insufficient insulin is produced, the body's cells do not absorb the glucose (sugar) they need for energy, and the liver does not store the excess sugar. This disease, *diabetes mellitus* [dī′ə•bē′tĭs mə•lī′təs], causes the unused sugar to collect in the blood. If the amount of sugar in the blood becomes too high, it overloads the brain and could cause a coma [kō′mə: unconsciousness].

Your pancreas also produces **pancreatic** [păng′krē•ăt′ĭk] **juice,** which pours through a duct into your small intestine. Pancreatic juice digests carbohydrates, proteins, and fats. Another function of your pancreas is to produce a substance that destroys the acid in the gastric juice so that the digestive juices in your small intestine can do their work.

Quick Checkup

Who am I?

1. I am a 20-foot-long coiled tube of muscles.
   small intestine

2. Most of the food you eat is digested in me.
   small intestine

3. I am the largest organ inside your body.
   liver

4. I am a greenish-colored digestive juice produced by your liver.
   bile

5. I store the digestive juice your liver produces.
   gallbladder

6. I am located between your stomach and small intestine.
   pancreas

7. I am a disease caused when too little insulin is produced.
   diabetes

8. I am the digestive juice that the pancreas produces.
   pancreatic juice

Absorbing digested food

Digested food must enter your bloodstream before it can nourish your body. Most nutrients from the food you eat enter your bloodstream from your small intestine. Millions of tiny, fingerlike projections called **villi** [vĭl′ī] stick out into the intestines. These villi are in the path of the digested food as it moves along. When food is digested so that it can dissolve in water, it passes through the thin walls of the villi and into the capillaries.

By the time food reaches the lower end of your small intestine, most of the nutrients that can be used have been absorbed into your bloodstream and are

villi on the intestinal wall

carried to the different parts of your body. The dissolved food that is not needed right away is changed by the liver into forms that can be stored until it is needed. Some of the food is stored in the liver, and some is stored under the skin as fat.

Eliminating unused food

Muscular contractions of your small intestine force the remainder of the food into your large intestine, or **colon,** which is twice as wide as your small intestine, but only about five feet long. The colon is made of muscles that continue to move food through the alimentary canal automatically.

Fiber, the rough parts of some fruits, vegetables, and grains, cannot be broken down and softened as it passes through the alimentary canal—it cannot be digested. The purpose of this unused part of the food in the diet is to clean the intestinal walls. The fiber is stored temporarily in the colon, where water and minerals are taken from the food and sent back into the bloodstream. Vitamins that

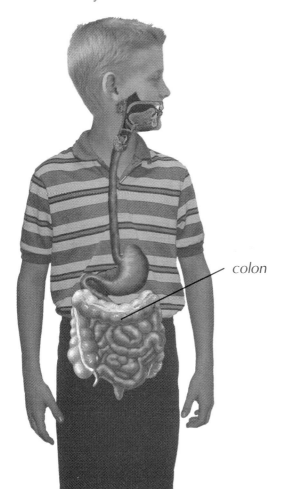

colon

Fiber-Rich Foods

are produced by bacteria in the colon are taken into the bloodstream with the water and minerals.

You need to *eat some fiber every day* to help your body get rid of waste materials. Recent studies have shown that people who eat a large amount of fiber have less chance of getting cancer of the colon. Good sources of fiber include *whole-grain breads and cereals, bran, raw fruits and vegetables, fruits with seeds* (such as figs and berries), and *nuts.* Some fiber is lost from fruits and vegetables when they are peeled. When flour is refined, nutrients as well as fiber are removed. Remember that whole-grain breads and cereals contain more vitamins, minerals, and fiber than white breads or refined cereals.

In order to keep your body healthy, the unusable part of the food or waste material must be removed from your body. When the waste material reaches the lower end of the colon, it is in a solid form and will be eliminated (sent out) from the body by the movement of the muscles in the colon. The passing of waste materials from the colon is sometimes referred to as a bowel (intestine) movement. From the time food is eaten until the unused part is eliminated takes from 24 to 48 hours.

Quick Checkup

Who am I?

1. Digested food must enter me before it can nourish your body.
   bloodstream

2. We are tiny, fingerlike projections in the small intestine.
   villi

3. I am a wide tube of muscles connected to your small intestine.
   colon (large intestine)

4. I help clean your intestinal walls.
   fiber

The importance of water

Over two thirds of your body is made up of water. Every part of your body contains some water—and every cell of your body needs water to do its work. Although you can stay alive for weeks without food, you can live only a few days without water. Your body loses about two quarts of water every day through breathing, perspiring, and the elimination of wastes. This water must be replaced in order for your body to function efficiently.

You get some water from the foods you eat. Soup, milk, and fruit and vegetable juices contain large amounts of water; even dried foods such as beans, rice, and oatmeal contain some water. Foods that are cooked for a short period of time contain more water than overcooked foods. Since your body does not store water, you need to drink several glasses of liquids each day. Most of these liquids should be *milk, fruit juices,* and *vegetable juices,* which are nourishing to your body, but you also need to drink *water.*

Water helps to keep your body clean inside by carrying away wastes. You need to drink enough liquids to replace the water that you lose in getting rid of wastes. If you do not drink enough liquids, your blood draws water from your body tissues, and your skin becomes dry. Also, your body cannot digest food or remove wastes properly with insufficient water. You may even get a stomachache or become constipated. Constipation results when your body fails to remove the solid waste part of the food from your intestines for several days.

Drinking sufficient liquids

You probably do not get enough liquids unless you drink water or juices between meals. Chewing gum can cause you to not feel thirsty and thus not to drink enough water. If you breathe through your mouth instead of your nose, you will get used to your mouth feeling dry. In cold weather, you may not drink enough liquids because you do not feel thirsty. You need to drink sufficient water, even if you do not feel thirsty, to help prevent colds and diseases.

You need to drink even more liquids in hot weather, because your body loses more water through perspiration. During moderate exercise in normal summer weather, you lose from one to two pints of water an hour. Drinking liquids, such as soft drinks, which contain caffeine can cause your body to lose water even faster. As you lose water, your body can no longer regulate your body temperature. Losing excessive amounts of water can result in fainting and heatstroke. Water that is lost in perspiration should be replaced as soon as possible to prevent fatigue.

Drinks that contain sugar are not absorbed by your body as quickly as water. Cool water helps quench your thirst, but it is not good to drink a lot of ice water in hot weather. When you do drink ice water, sip it slowly.

Additional liquids are required for sick persons with a fever, vomiting, or diarrhea. The body also needs extra liquids if large amounts of salt or sugar have been eaten.

Healthful Hint

Drinking sufficient liquids helps your body in many ways.

- It helps control your body temperature.
- It carries nutrients to your body.
- It helps the digestion of your food.
- It helps change food into energy.
- It is needed to produce blood, saliva, and digestive juices.
- It carries wastes from your body.

Making drinking water safe

Over 100 years ago, as a result of the rapid spreading of the disease typhoid fever, a young scientist named William Sedgwick was able to show that impure drinking water caused the disease to spread from one town to another along the Merrimac River in the northwestern part of the United States.

In most cities, after water is taken from a river or another source, it is piped to a treatment plant and mixed with chemicals. Bacteria, mud, and other impurities stick to the chemicals and settle to the bottom; then the water is passed through more than three feet of sand and gravel to filter out any remaining particles. The water then flows to a huge reservoir (place of storage), where a substance called chlorine is added to kill remaining bacteria. Most communities add chlorine to their water, even if they do not purify it any other way.

Dysentery [dĭs′ən·tĕr′ē], a painful infection of the colon, is sometimes caused by water that has become polluted by sewage and other impurities. If you travel to parts of the world where the ordinary drinking water is not purified, you will need to be very careful to drink only purified water.

Some liquids are harmful

Because there is no food value besides Calories in soft drinks, tea, and coffee, they are not a good source of liquids. If you drink much tea or soft drinks, you probably are not drinking as much milk as your body needs for growing strong bones and teeth. Most coffee and tea and many soft drinks contain *caffeine,* a drug that is not good for your body while you are still growing. If you drink a 12-ounce can of cola, you get as much caffeine in relation to your body size as an adult who drinks three or more cups of coffee.

Caffeine affects your nervous system and makes you feel as if you have more energy than you really have. It can make you restless at school and keep you from sleeping soundly at night. Since your body grows and repairs itself when you sleep, you should not drink anything that will keep you from getting the sleep you

need. Excessive amounts of caffeine can result in high blood pressure.

Caffeine also acts as a drug, forcing the kidneys to give up too much water. In addition, all soft drinks contain much acid, giving a tingling sensation which you feel in your mouth. Drinking or eating many high-acid foods makes your kidneys work harder, because the kidneys must expel the extra acids into the urine. Because of the high-acid content of soft drinks, drinking too many of them can damage your kidneys.

Alcohol is a liquid that is extremely harmful to the body. It weakens the body so that it cannot fight disease. It affects the brain so that a person is unable to see properly, unable to walk steadily, and unable to think or talk clearly. It is the cause of many accidents and deaths. And it has an even greater effect on children with their smaller body size than it has on adults.

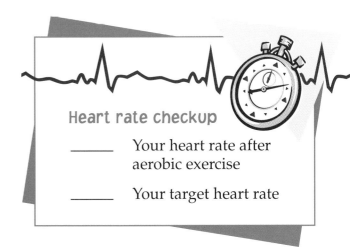

Heart rate checkup

_____ Your heart rate after aerobic exercise

_____ Your target heart rate

Additional aids to digestion

Your digestive system works better when you *eat your meals at regular times,* because then it is given plenty of time for rest. You feel better, too, when you eat at regular times. If you have to go without food until after your regular mealtime, you probably become tired and maybe even cross.

In addition to drinking sufficient water and eating fruits, vegetables, and grains containing fiber, *your body needs exercise* in order to eliminate body wastes properly. However, you may want to relax for awhile before and after meals.

Overeating is harmful

Eating too much food at one time overworks the digestive system. If the stomach is too full, no room is left for the stomach muscles to mash, squeeze, press, and churn the food and digestive juices together. You feel uncomfortable, and you may even get a stomachache or a headache.

Quick Checkup
True/False

1. Only one third of your body is made up of water.
   false

2. You need liquids only at mealtimes.
   false

3. Persons with a fever, vomiting, or diarrhea need more liquids than usual.
   true

4. Dysentery is an infection of the colon.
   true

5. Alcohol affects a person's brain.
   true

When you gulp your food or eat too fast, you are more likely to overeat and less likely to chew your food well. Eating slowly lowers your chances of eating too much and gaining excess weight. No matter how much food you eat, your body will use only the part it needs for energy, for growth, and for repair. The remainder of the food will be stored as fat.

Your feelings affect digestion

In 1895 a nine-year-old boy, now known only as Tom, swallowed some steaming-hot clam chowder. The chowder seared his esophagus and blocked the passageway to his stomach. Tom was rushed to the hospital, but efforts to unblock his esophagus failed. Although Tom recovered, he was left with an opening an inch and a half wide into his stomach.

As time passed, only Tom's family and a few close friends knew of the hole in his stomach. One day over 40 years later while Tom was digging ditches, the lifting of a heavy pick every few seconds caused the bandage to rub continually against the opening, making it bleed. When Tom arrived at a hospital, the doctors immediately realized they had an opportunity to learn even more about the stomach. They observed that whenever Tom was sad or fearful, gastric juice stopped flowing into his stomach. Whenever Tom felt resentful or angry, excess digestive juices flooded into his stomach.

Healthful Hint

Relax and enjoy your meal.

The doctors concluded that if too much acid is produced by the stomach, some of the excess acid may be carried up the esophagus with a gas bubble. This can cause *heartburn*—a pain or burning behind the breastbone and a sour taste in the mouth. The pain from heartburn is even worse if you lie down. Sometimes excess acid may go with the food into the small intestine where it can cause a *peptic ulcer*—an open sore in the alimentary canal.

Quick Checkup
- ☐ I always chew my food thoroughly.
- ☐ I eat at regular times.
- ☐ I avoid overeating.
- ☐ I help keep mealtimes pleasant.

First Base

Outdoor games combine muscle-building exercise with the benefits of fresh air and sunshine. First Base, which may be played by either a large or a small group, strengthens batting, throwing, and running skills. These are important skills for softball and baseball.

To play First Base, you need a softball field or a large playing field. If you are not using a softball field, the equipment you need includes a **base and home plate** in addition to a **bat** and a **softball** or small rubber ball. The baselines to the left and right of home plate are **foul lines.**

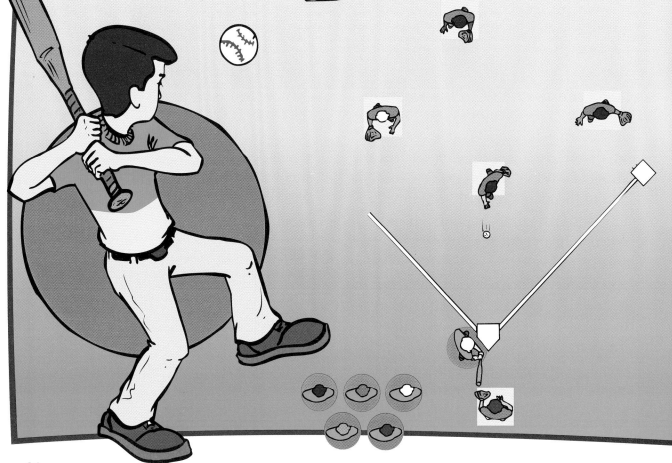

Divide into two equal teams, making sure that each team has a catcher, a pitcher, and at least three fielders. One team begins at home plate; the other begins in the field. The players at home plate take turns batting the ball. The pitcher throws the ball underhand to the batter, and the batter hits the ball as hard as he can into the field. After he hits the ball, the batter runs to first base and back to home plate without stopping.

Any player from the team in the field may catch the ball. If the ball is caught before it touches the ground, the batter is out. If the ball has bounced or is rolling on the ground, a fielder catches the ball and throws it to the catcher. If the catcher, while holding the ball, can touch home plate with his foot before the batter gets back to home plate, the batter is out.

If the batter swings but misses the ball, he has a strike against him. A batter also gets a strike if he hits the ball outside the foul lines. If a batter gets three strikes, he is out. When three people on a team make outs, the teams change places. Each team should have the same number of chances to bat. Every time a batter runs to first base and back to home plate without making an out, he scores a point for his team.

Keeping mealtimes pleasant

Just as excitement, anger, and fear at mealtime can cause you to get a stomachache, headache, or heartburn, so happy thoughts and feelings will help you to have good digestion. Therefore, keeping every mealtime a pleasant, relaxing time is really a good health habit.

Anytime that you think of others, your mealtimes will be more pleasant. You will *always be on time to meals* if you do not want to make others wait. Do you *comb your hair and wash your hands and face* before you come to the table, or do you have to be reminded? Remember that your appearance should be pleasant to others. Also, washing your hands does more than improve your appearance. Soap and warm water wash away germs that can pass from your dirty hands through your mouth to your intestines, making you sick.

You should *stand behind your chair until everyone is ready* to be seated.

Healthful Hint

Don't lick your fingers.

Since the men seat the women, the women sit down first. Boys, do you ever seat your teacher at school or seat your mother when your father is away? If you have never seated anyone before, practice it at home with your mother. Stand behind the chair and pull it out far enough that she can get between the chair and the table. When she bends her knees to sit, push the chair forward gently. As you sit in your own seat, be careful not to jar the table.

After you *thank God for your food,* you should *put your napkin on your lap.* A large napkin should be left folded in half. Use your napkin whenever you need to wipe your mouth or fingers. After you use your napkin, put it on your lap again—no one likes to look at a messy napkin on the table. You should not stick gum on your plate nor put it in a cloth napkin. And, of course, never use a cloth napkin as a handkerchief.

Do you *wait for the food to be passed* to you? You should never reach across the table for it. When food is passed around the table, it is usually passed to the right. Whenever you dish food onto your plate, be sure that you use only the serving spoon. Serve yourself from the food that is closest to you, as it is never polite to reach across a dish for the largest piece of something. Try to put on your plate only as much food as you will eat. Of course, you will want to *take a little bit of every food that is served.* Your mother spends time preparing a variety of appetizing foods so that you can have a balanced diet. If you do not eat some of everything, you will not get all the nutrients that your body needs. If a new food or a food that you do not like is being served, to be polite you should eat at least two or three bites of it. By eating a little bit every time the food is served, you can learn to like most foods.

Healthful Hint

You can learn to like a food by eating a little each time it's served.

After you have served yourself, be sure to pass the food on. You should wait to eat until your mother or the hostess begins eating; at school, your teacher should begin eating first if she or he sits at your table. While you are eating, do you have good posture? Good posture keeps the parts of your digestive system from being crowded so that they can function properly. You should sit straight and tall, and *keep the hand that you are not using in your lap.* It is not polite to eat with your elbows on the table.

Do you know how to hold your fork and spoon when you are eating? Most foods are eaten with a fork. Fill the fork about halfway up the prongs, and eat the food from the points of the prongs; never eat from the side of a fork. Always *swallow the food that is in your mouth before you take another bite.*

How do you hold your fork and knife to cut meat? If you are right-handed, hold the fork in your left hand and the knife in your right hand. You hold the meat in place with the fork and cut it with the knife. Do not cut all of your meat at one time; cut only one or two pieces at a time as you eat your meal.

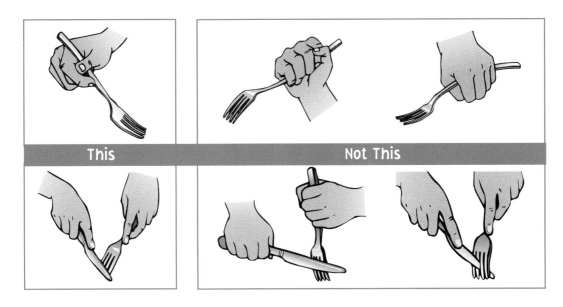

This | Not This

Swallow the food in your mouth before you take a drink.

Swallow before you talk, too!

While you are cutting, your elbows should be kept near your sides so that you will not bump someone sitting next to you. If you are sitting too close to the table, you will not be able to keep your elbows near your sides as you cut.

When you eat soup, spoon it away from you and take it into your mouth from the side of the spoon. You should *never slurp soup* or drink it from the bowl. It is never polite to scoop food onto your fork with your thumb or fingers or to clean food from your plate with your fingers. You should always keep your food on your plate rather than on the table beside your plate. Bread is easier to eat if you break a small piece from the slice and butter it instead of buttering a whole slice and taking bites from it. Rolls and biscuits should be eaten the same way. Do not spit seeds or bones out of your mouth; carefully take them out with your finger and thumb. Of course, you should never lick your knife. It is also impolite to make gestures with your eating utensils as you talk.

You and everyone around you will be more comfortable if you *use your eating utensils correctly.*

Do you ever take such large bites of food that you have trouble chewing it? You should not stuff your mouth with food: *take small bites* so that you can chew your food well. Remember—chewing your food well helps your food to digest better. Always swallow the food in your mouth before you take a drink so that you do not wash down some of the food before it is chewed well and so that small pieces of food will not be left in your drink. Food floating in your drink is not pleasant for others to look at. Wipe your lips carefully with your napkin after you have finished drinking. You should always *chew with your mouth closed*— you look better, and you sound better, too. Never talk with food in your mouth; this makes it difficult to understand what you are saying, and no one wants to see inside your mouth.

Quick Checkup

- ☐ I am on time for breakfast.
- ☐ I am on time for dinner or supper.
- ☐ I wait for food to be passed to me.
- ☐ I keep my napkin on my lap.
- ☐ I eat a little of every food that is served.
- ☐ I always chew with my mouth closed.
- ☐ I never talk with food in my mouth.

Healthful Habits

Good habits for good digestion.

- Chew your food thoroughly.
- Do not overeat.
- Eat at regular times.
- Eat foods containing fiber every day.
- Drink at least six large glasses of liquids daily.
- Exercise regularly.
- Relax for awhile before and after meals.
- Keep your mealtimes pleasant.

Another way to help others enjoy their food is to **talk about pleasant things.** The time to discuss problems is not at the table. Speaking in a quiet, cheerful voice is helpful, too. So is the ability to wait for your turn before you talk; you should **never interrupt** another person. It is always courteous to listen to what others have to say. Of course, you should never say anything unpleasant about the food. If seconds are served, say, **"No, thank you,"** if you do not care for any more. If you want something passed to you, you should always say **"please."** Do you remember to say **"thank you"** after it has been passed? When someone asks you to pass something, be sure you pass the serving dish; do not just hand the food, such as a carrot stick or a cookie, to him. If an accident happens at the table, such as spilling your drink or breaking a dish, apologize to the hostess. If you are at home, apologize and then help clean it up. When it is necessary to leave the table before the meal is finished, ask to be excused, saying, "May I be excused, please?" or "Please excuse me."

Your mother works hard to prepare attractive, nutritious meals. Do you remember to tell her "thank you"? When you are finished eating, place your eating utensils on your plate and lay your napkin neatly to the left of your plate; do not fold the napkin. Then **wait patiently at the table until you are excused.** It is impolite to run your tongue around your mouth to remove particles of food or to leave the table while you still have food in your mouth. After you have been excused, quietly get up from the table and **push in your chair.** If it is your job to help with the dishes, begin right away.

Healthful Hint

Don't talk about problems at the table.

Comprehension Checkup

I. **ANATOMY PURSUIT:** Complete the puzzle to find out the name of the tube through your body in which food is broken down.

1. the back teeth that grind food

2. where bile is stored

3. fingerlike projections in the intestines that absorb food

4. where food is stored before it is digested

5. the largest organ inside the body

6. a front tooth

7. most food is digested in the small __?__

8. a long tube that connects the mouth to the stomach

9. where insulin and pancreatic juice are produced

10. the throat

11. a tooth with two cusps

12. the windpipe

13. carries the waste parts of food from the body

14. a digestive juice in the mouth

15. a tiny flap of cartilage that covers the trachea during swallowing

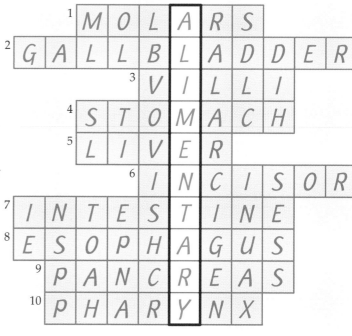

1. MOLARS
2. GALLBLADDER
3. VILLI
4. STOMACH
5. LIVER
6. INCISOR
7. INTESTINE
8. ESOPHAGUS
9. PANCREAS
10. PHARYNX

11. BICUSPID
12. TRACHEA
13. COLON
14. SALIVA
15. EPIGLOTTIS

II. COMPLETION: Write the correct answers on the lines.

digestion   1. The breaking down of food into a form the body can use is called ＿?＿.

absorption   2. The process that makes food available to your body is called ＿?＿.

fiber   3. The rough parts of some foods that cannot be digested are ＿?＿.

kidney   4. A bean-shaped organ about the size of your fist is a ＿?＿.

III. LISTING: Write three important functions of the liver.

1. _recycles iron, stores sugar_

2. _produces bile, removes wastes_

3. _stores vitamins and minerals_

IV. IDENTIFICATION: Write the digestive juice beside its place of function.

saliva	1. mouth	bile
gastric juice	2. stomach	gastric juice
bile	3. small intestine	pancreatic juice
pancreatic juice	4. small intestine	saliva

V. EVALUATION

1. Name two times you should drink additional liquids.

   during hot weather; after strenuous exercise;
   if you are sick with a fever, vomiting, or diarrhea

2. Name four good health habits you practice that aid good digestion.

   See page 85.

Physical Fitness in Action

Statistics show that the average American child today is not in as good physical condition as children in days gone by. This is blamed largely on spending long periods of time watching television instead of enjoying healthful outdoor exercise. What is your physical fitness rating? Besides your physical education classes at school, do you exercise often, seldom, or hardly ever?

Being physically fit has many advantages, from helping you control your weight to giving you a restful night's sleep. It helps you look and feel well. And even more important, research shows that those who exercise regularly are less likely to get such "killer" diseases as heart attacks and strokes.

Fitness factors

Overall physical fitness is based on *aerobic endurance, muscular strength and endurance, agility, flexibility,* and *body composition.* If you are physically fit, you are full of energy for performing your daily activities and are enthusiastic about learning new forms of active recreation.

Warming up gradually

Our bodies are designed for movement, but when you first get up in the morning or stand after sitting for a long time, you may feel stiff and sluggish. Stretching makes you feel alert and ready to go. Stretching before you begin many activities also benefits your body. Proper stretching lengthens your muscles, tendons, and connective tissue. You should always *stretch slowly—just to the point of tightness—and hold the stretch for 15–30 seconds.* Stretching to the point of pain means injury and loss of flexibility. *Never bounce or jerk while stretching,* since this could cause you to overstretch, injuring a muscle or tendon.

Before you begin any strenuous game or activity, your body needs to warm up. **Warm-ups** are light exercises that send warm blood flowing to your muscles, raising the temperature of the muscles that are used. Because the warmth from the increased circulation makes your muscles looser and more elastic, there is less chance of injury. If you begin vigorous exercise before your muscles are warmed up, you will end up with sore muscles, possible strains, or torn ligaments. Light exercises also speed up the work of your heart and lungs and prepare them for more strenuous exercise. Warm-ups could include stretching exercises, bike riding, fast walking, or slow jogging.

Healthful Hint

During a warm-up jog, stay flat footed as much as possible to let the tendons in your feet and ankles stretch gradually.

Cooling off slowly

Properly caring for your muscles also means allowing them to cool down and return to normal once you have finished any strenuous exercise. You should gradually decrease the intensity of your activity until both your heart rate and breathing have slowed down. You should always stretch again *after* energetic exercise—it helps reduce stiffness and soreness.

As you check your level of fitness in the areas of muscular strength and endurance, agility, and flexibility, be sure you begin by stretching the muscles you will be using. Before doing an aerobic activity, you may want to do additional warm-ups. Remember to stretch again when you are finished.

Quick Checkup
True/False

1. When touching your toes, you should stretch slowly and hold the stretch.
   true

2. Warm-ups send more blood to your muscles.
   true

3. Cooling off after strenuous exercise causes stiffnessand soreness.
   false

4. Your physical fitness depends on your ability to play sports.
   false

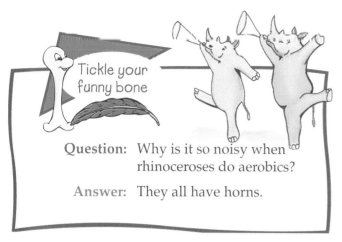
Aerobic endurance

The term *aerobic* refers to the presence of oxygen. God has provided you with an amazing body system that brings life-giving oxygen into your body—your **respiratory system.** Refer to the illustration on page 96 and list the parts of the respiratory system as you follow the passageway for air from the nose or mouth to the lungs.

When you exercise, your body needs more oxygen. Have you noticed that you breathe more deeply during heavy exercise? **Aerobics** are exercises that help your body process large amounts of oxygen efficiently. Aerobic exercise, **continuous activity without rest,** builds your endurance by strengthening your heart and lungs as well as your skeletal muscles. Studies show that *you need aerobic exercise at least 20 to 30 minutes three times a week.*

Measuring a Lungful

To compare the amount of air you use in a single breath before and after you exercise, you will need *a glass gallon jug, a tape measure, a large basin or bowl, and a 2-foot length of rubber tubing.*

Fill the jug with water. Then cover the mouth of the jug with your hand and place the jug, upside down, into the large basin (or bowl) half full of water. Slip one end of the rubber tube into the neck of the jug while someone holds the jug slightly above the bottom of the basin. Without taking a deep breath, exhale one full breath through the rubber tube.

The space above the water contains the air that you exhaled. How far down did the water level go? Measure the distance that the water went down.

Refill the jug and place it back in the basin. Now exercise vigorously for several minutes. While you are still puffing and panting, exhale one full breath through the tube. How far down does the water level go this time? Measure again and compare this measurement with the first one. How does exercise affect your breathing? Not exercising your lungs enough can cause you to have a flat chest and rounded shoulders.

Fitness for a Lifetime

To maintain or increase your aerobic endurance, **you need aerobic exercise at least three times each week** for the remainder of your life. An endurance run involves large-muscle, whole-body activity for an extended period of time. Using a **stopwatch,** time yourself while you jog or run one mile. If you become tired, rest while you walk a short distance and then resume running or jogging.

Regularly complete the endurance run to check your level of aerobic endurance. Record the time it takes you to finish each run, trying to improve your personal best until you can repeatedly finish in your recommended amount of time. Also record your heart rate. Each time you reach your target heart rate, circle your heart rate with a red pen or pencil. Congratulations!

Date	Fitness activity	Minutes	Heart rate	Target heart rate

Healthful Hint

Exercise regularly.

Quick Checkup

Name the terms.

1. Refers to the presence of oxygen
   aerobic
2. The body system that takes in air
   respiratory
3. The number of times a week you need aerobic exercise
   at least three
4. The body parts that aerobics strengthen
   heart, lungs, skeletal muscles

Respiratory system

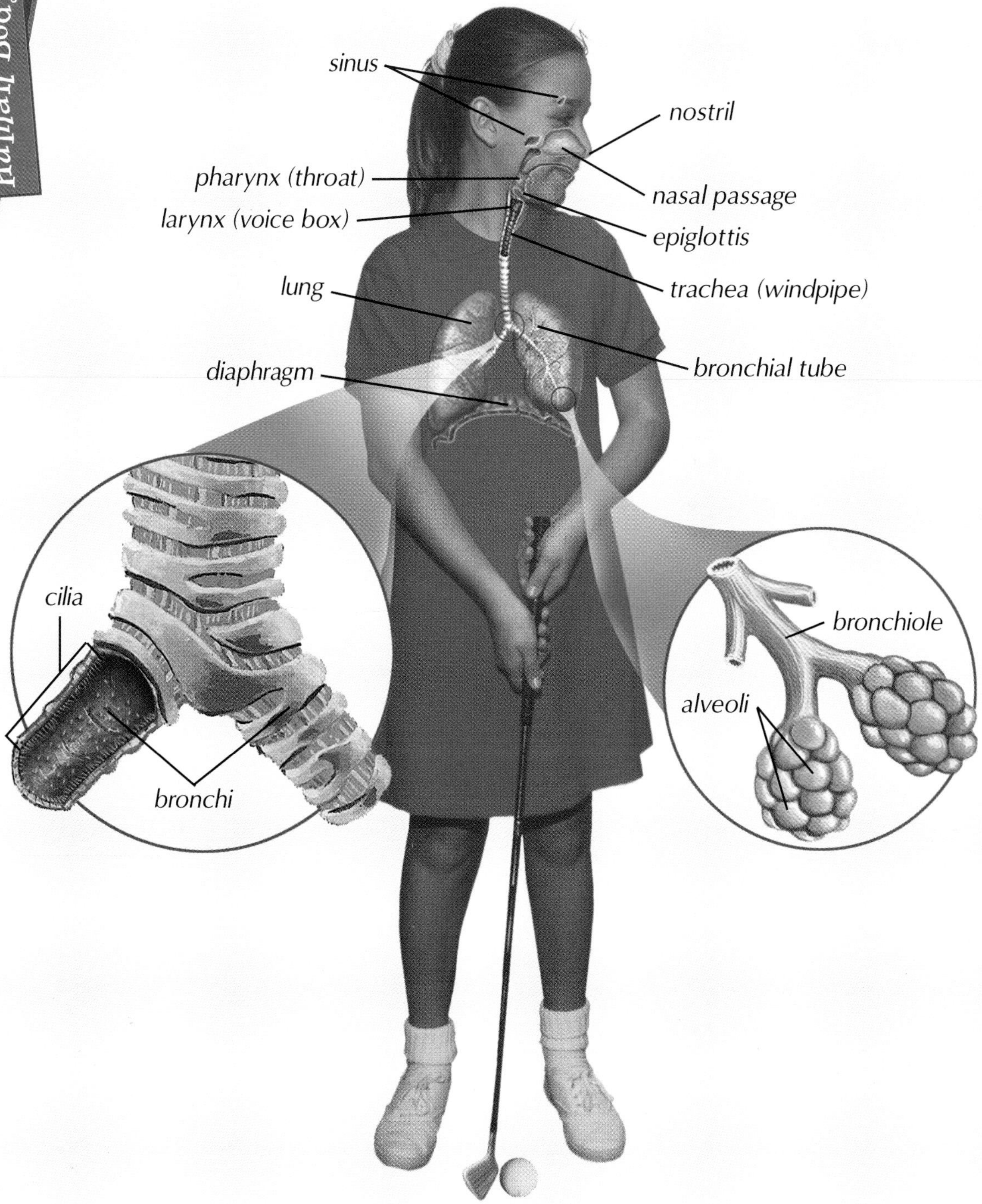

sinus

nostril

pharynx (throat)

nasal passage

larynx (voice box)

epiglottis

lung

trachea (windpipe)

diaphragm

bronchial tube

cilia

bronchi

bronchiole

alveoli

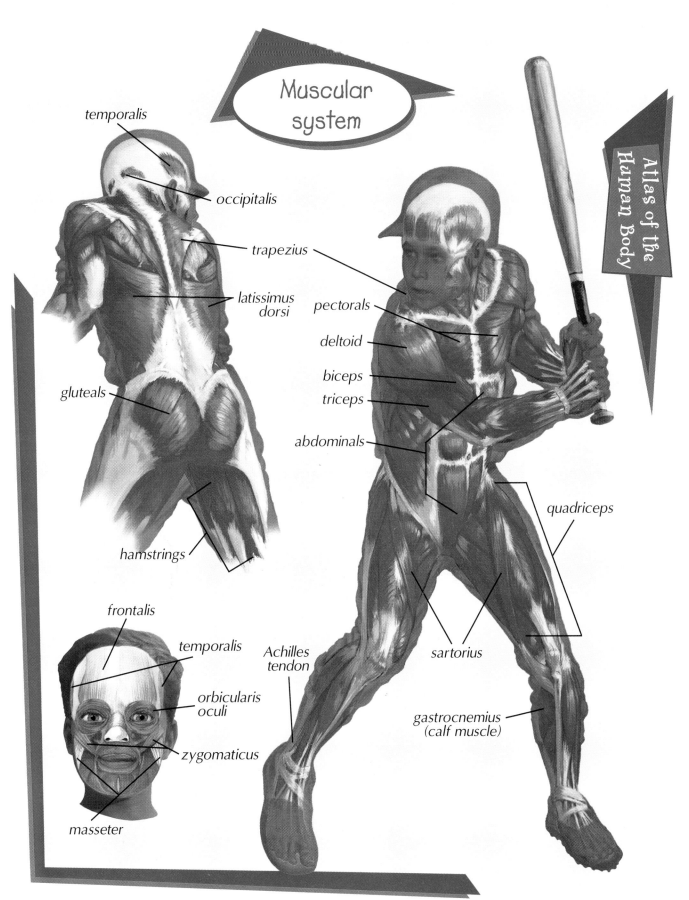

Muscular system

temporalis

occipitalis

trapezius

latissimus dorsi

pectorals

deltoid

biceps

triceps

abdominals

gluteals

quadriceps

hamstrings

frontalis

temporalis

Achilles tendon

orbicularis oculi

sartorius

zygomaticus

gastrocnemius (calf muscle)

masseter

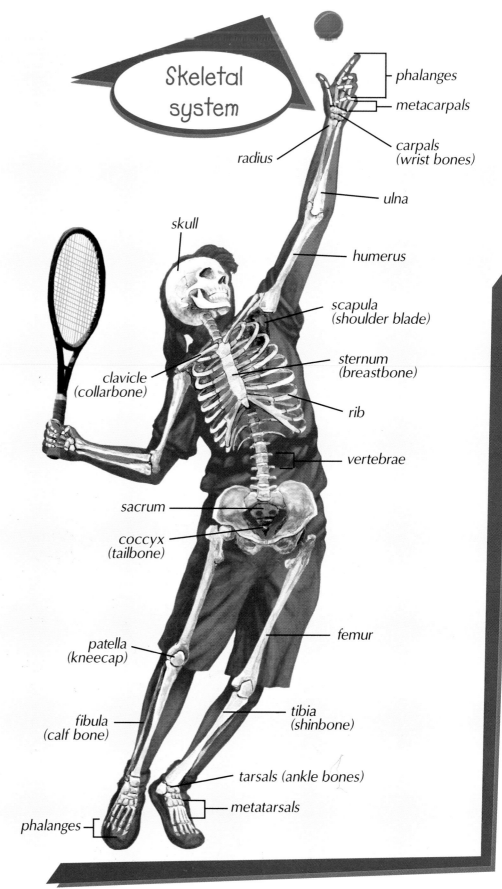

Skeletal system

phalanges

metacarpals

carpals (wrist bones)

radius

ulna

humerus

skull

scapula (shoulder blade)

sternum (breastbone)

rib

clavicle (collarbone)

vertebrae

sacrum

coccyx (tailbone)

femur

patella (kneecap)

fibula (calf bone)

tibia (shinbone)

tarsals (ankle bones)

metatarsals

phalanges

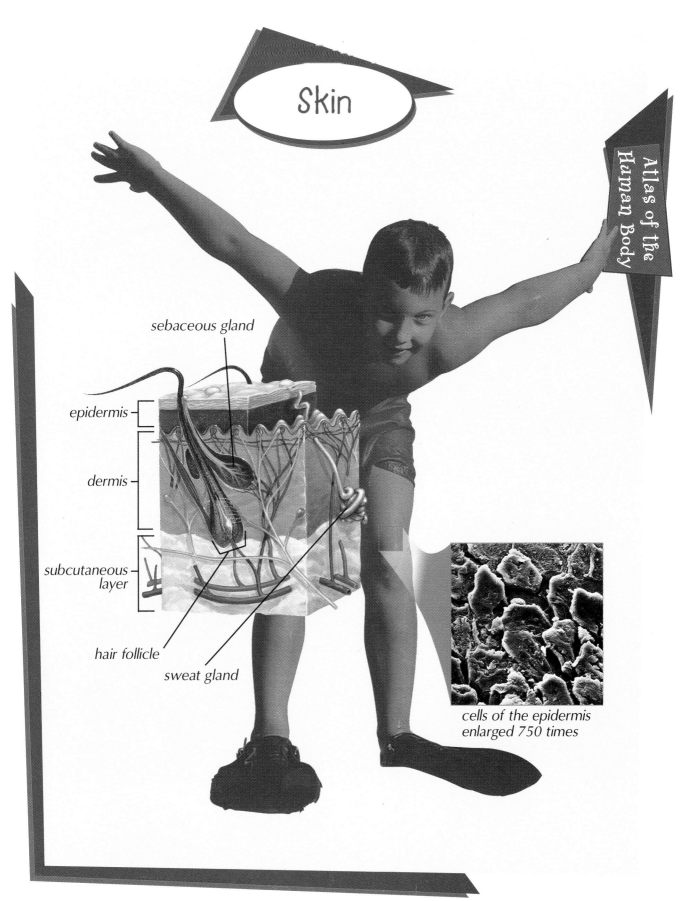

Skin

sebaceous gland

epidermis

dermis

subcutaneous layer

hair follicle

sweat gland

cells of the epidermis
enlarged 750 times

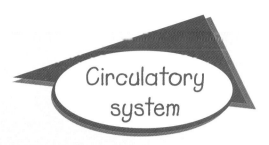

Circulatory system

Follow the path of blood from the right atrium to the right ventricle, the left lung, the left atrium, the left ventricle, and out through the aorta to all parts of the body.

left lung

right lung

A
E
I
F
F
B
C
G
H
D

A. aorta

B. left atrium

C. left ventricle

D. lower vena cava

E. pulmonary artery
(to the lungs)

F. pulmonary veins
(from the lungs)

G. right atrium

H. right ventricle

I. upper vena cava

aorta

upper vena cava

pulmonary artery
(supplies blood
to the lungs)

cardiac muscle
(heart)

lower vena cava

arteries
(carry blood
from the heart)

veins
(carry blood back
to the heart)

Digestive
system

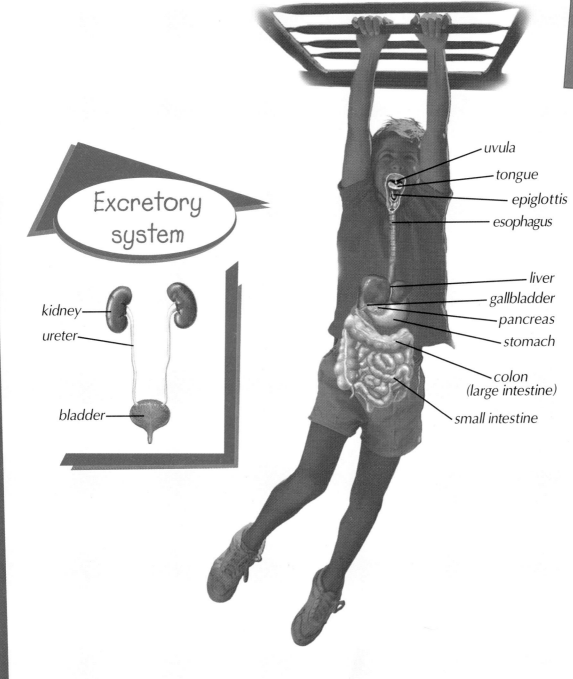

Excretory
system

kidney

ureter

bladder

uvula

tongue

epiglottis

esophagus

liver

gallbladder

pancreas

stomach

colon
(large intestine)

small intestine

Muscular strength and endurance

Use it or lose it

What would happen if you lay in bed all day and never moved your body? Your muscles would become flabby, your circulation sluggish, and your bones weak. Doctors urge even patients who have had serious surgery to exercise as soon as they are able to stagger out of bed with the help of nurses. Moving their bodies is essential to their recovery. In cases where patients must stay in bed or in a wheel chair, specially trained people called **physical therapists** [thĕr′ə·pĭsts] exercise their muscles for them by moving their muscles and joints until they can do this themselves. Most of you do not need physical therapists—you can move your own body. But do you? Remember, you need aerobic exercise at least three days a week.

Where the action is

Skeletal muscles (muscles connected to the skeleton) are made up of thousands of thin, long fibers, or cells, which are bundled together. The longest muscle in your body, the **sartorius,** stretches from the outside of your hip to the inside of your knee. Can you locate it on the illustration of the *muscular system* on page 97? Your facial muscles allow you to move your lower jaw when you eat, to move your lips when you talk or sing, and to show emotion.

When you lock your elbow and raise your arm, you use your **deltoid** muscle. Try it. Put your left hand on your right shoulder, lock your right elbow, and raise your right arm away from your side. Lower your arm, and with your elbow still locked, raise your right arm in front

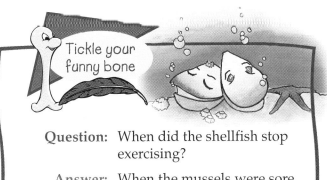

Tickle your funny bone

Question: When did the shellfish stop exercising?

Answer: When the mussels were sore.

Exercise is vital for strong muscles. Most body tissues grow as the cells divide to make new cells. But muscle fibers (cells) do not divide. When your muscles are exercised regularly, your heart supplies them with more blood and nutrients to make the fibers thicker. Thus, *the more muscles are used, the larger and stronger they become.*

of you. Do you feel the movement of the deltoid under your left hand? Now bend your elbow and raise and lower your right lower arm. Which muscles in your upper arm do you feel contracting and relaxing? Turn again to the illustration of the muscular system to see if your answer is correct.

Next, move your leg or another part of your body. Then, on the illustration of the muscular system, try to find the muscle which causes that motion. Touch that muscle on your body as you make the same movement again. Did you choose the right muscle? Can you feel the muscle shorten and thicken with the movement? As you do the opposite movement, does the muscle become long and thin again?

Quick Checkup
Name the terms.
1. The longest muscle in your body
   sartorius
2. A muscle which helps you raise your arm
   deltoid
3. One who is specially trained to exercise another person's muscles
   physical therapist
4. What exercise does for muscles
   strengthens, enlarges
5. The ability of muscles to continue producing moderate strength for an extended time
   muscular endurance (See p. 104.)

Your **muscular strength** is the ability of your muscles to produce a great amount of strength for a short period of time. Your **muscular endurance** is the ability of your muscles to continue producing a moderate amount of strength for an extended period of time.

Come on, guys. With no rest in between, let's show them we can do at least two.

Girls, we have to do only one.

Pull-ups

Let's test the **muscular strength and endurance of your upper body** (upper arms and shoulders). Begin by grasping a **horizontal bar** with your palms facing either toward or away from your body. Hang from the bar with your arms and legs extended but your feet not touching the ground. From this hanging position, pull your body up until your chin is above the bar and then return to the hanging position.

Standing Long Jump

To test your **lower body strength,** tape a **line** on the floor and then tape a **measuring tape** to the floor at a right angle to the line. Stand with your toes behind the line and your feet slightly apart. Just before jumping, bend your knees and swing your arms backward. As you push off with your legs, swing your arms forward. The length of your jump is measured from the line to the back of your heel (or other part of your body that touches the floor nearest the line).

Standing Long Jump

Age	Girls	Boys
10	4' 5 "	4' 11"
11	4' 9"	5' 1"
12	5' 1"	5' 4"

Curl-ups

To test the **muscular strength and endurance of your abdominals,** lie on your back on a **mat** (or other appropriate surface) with your knees bent and your feet on the mat. Cross your arms, placing your hands on the opposite shoulders, and tuck your chin close to your chest. Keeping your arms against your chest, curl up until your elbows touch your thighs. Then uncurl until the middle of your back touches the mat. Have someone hold your feet only when you are being tested.

Complete as many curl-ups as possible in 60 seconds. If necessary, you may rest between curl-ups in either the up or down position. But you may not count incorrect curl-ups—your arms leaving your chest, your hands leaving your shoulders, your knees straightening, or the middle of your back not touching the mat between curl-ups. Ready, set, GO!

Sit-ups

Age	Girls	Boys
10	30	34
11	33	36
12	33	38

Flexibility

Increasing in stature

When God created you, He "built in" a special, automatic activity. This activity—growth—continues until you are an adult. The way you are growing physically now is quite special. One year you may grow several inches, whereas the next year you may grow very little. God also made you with a "slow-down" activity. The older you become, the more slowly your size changes until finally in your teen years or your early twenties, you will stop growing taller. Most of your cells keep dividing and multiplying as long as you live, however, in order to replace worn-out cells. But the only change you will be able to make in your body size then is to gain or lose weight.

Tickle your funny bone

Question: How does a centipede stay physically fit?

Answer: By many feets of endurance.

Boning up

When you measure your increase in height, you actually are measuring how much taller your skeleton has grown. Your skeleton has 206 bones, all different sizes and shapes, and each one created for a definite purpose. Refer to the illustration of the *skeletal system* on page 98. Your bony **skull** is like a strong, built-in helmet. It protects your brain from

bumps and bruises. Your bony **ribs** form a cage that protects your heart and lungs. Your feet, having one fourth of the bones in your body, can carry you 70,000 miles—nearly three times around the world—in a single lifetime!

Your spinal column, made up of 24 vertebrae [vûr′tə·brā] plus the **sacrum** [sā′krəm] and the **coccyx** [kŏk′sĭks: tailbone], forms a long, bony tube which protects the delicate nerves of your spinal cord. Your vertebrae also help you stand up straight. But at the same time they allow you to bend, stoop, twist, and turn.

Besides supporting and protecting your body, some bones manufacture blood cells. They do this vital work in the **red marrow.** Because the red blood cells work constantly, they wear out

rapidly. At least three million red cells are worn out *every second!* But God designed your bone marrow to make new red blood cells at the same rate, about three million per second.

Quick Checkup
Name the terms.

1. I have 206 bones.
   skeleton

2. I protect your brain.
   skull

3. We protect your heart and lungs.
   ribs

4. I am your tailbone.
   coccyx

5. We help you to stand straight but also allow you to bend.
   vertebrae

6. I am the part of a bone where blood cells are manufactured.
   red marrow

Sit and Stretch

You know that exercise is important to keep muscles strong. But exercise is also important in keeping joints flexible. To measure your flexibility, tape a **line** on the floor and place a **yardstick** across it so that the line is even with the 12-inch mark.

Sit on the floor with your heels against the line and 12 inches apart. Keeping your legs straight, bend forward slowly with your fingertips sliding along the yardstick. Reach as far as you comfortably can, momentarily holding the stretch. Remember, you should **never bounce or jerk while stretching,** because overstretching means injury and loss of flexibility.

Repeat the stretch four times. If you reach short of your mark on your last try, doing the sit and stretch exercise regularly will increase the flexibility of your lower back and hamstring muscles.

Body composition

Skin cells complete their life cycle in about 27 days. If you look at a shaft of sunlight as it streams through a window, you will see tiny particles of dust and dead skin floating in the air. During your lifetime you will wash and scratch off more than 40 pounds of dead skin, and you will have approximately 1,000 new outer skins.

Refer to the illustration of the skin on page 99 to see which layer of skin dies and falls off. Which part of the skin is a layer of fat? Some body fat is essential—it covers nerves, coats the outside of cells, cushions many vital organs in your body, and during cold weather acts as an insulator, holding in your body heat. Most body fat is **subcutaneous fat,** the layer of skin where excess energy is stored. This layer of skin contains loose connective tissue which makes the skin flexible and connects it to the muscles.

Although some body fat is necessary, too much fat raises the body's risk of diseases related to *obesity* (being 20% or more overweight). Fat is living tissue that requires blood vessels for distributing food and oxygen. For every excess pound of fat, the heart must pump blood through an extra 200 miles of tiny capillaries. Think of the extra work a person's heart has if he is ten pounds overweight.

Fat formed in the body from overeating can also raise the level of a certain type of cholesterol (a fatty substance) in

Healthful Hint

Eating foods rich in fiber helps prevent cholesterol buildup.

the blood, causing even *greater risk of heart disease.* Too much of this cholesterol in the blood is especially harmful if a person smokes cigarettes or is overweight.

Quick Checkup
True/False

1. The epidermis is the layer of skin that flakes off.
   true

2. The dermis stores fat.
   false

3. Obesity is being 20% or more overweight.
   true

4. Body weight can be divided into fat and lean.
   true

5. Excess body fat decreases agility.
   true

Your Optimal Range

Your total body weight can be divided into fat and lean. Lean body mass includes bone, skin, hair, internal organs, muscles—everything but body fat. The thickness of a fold of skin over your **triceps** and **gastrocnemius** [găs′trŏk·nē′mĭ·əs] muscles can be measured by your teacher or another adult with *skinfold calipers* to determine your percentage of body fat.

The measurer grasps the skin on the back of your relaxed arm between his thumb and index finger. While holding the skinfold, he places the jaws of the calipers over the skinfold and releases the trigger. Still holding the skinfold between his thumb and index finger, he allows the jaws to exert their full tension for two seconds before reading the scale to the nearest 1.0 mm. Take three separate measurements and record your middle score.

Turn to the illustration of the muscles on page 97. Can you find the gastrocnemius muscle? This is the other muscle that is measured to determine your percentage of body fat. Place your foot on a bench or chair with your knee at a 90° angle. The measurer grasps the skin on the inside of your lower leg and measures the skinfold, again taking three separate measurements. Record your middle score and add this figure to your score taken from the triceps muscle.

Using the chart on page 111, determine if you are within the optimal range for body fat. The optimal (most healthful) fat content for boys is 10%–20% and for girls is 15%–27%. If you are *below the optimal range,* your growth of other tissues may be impaired. If you are *above the optimal range,* your risk of many diseases is greater.

Total of the skinfold measurements (in mm)

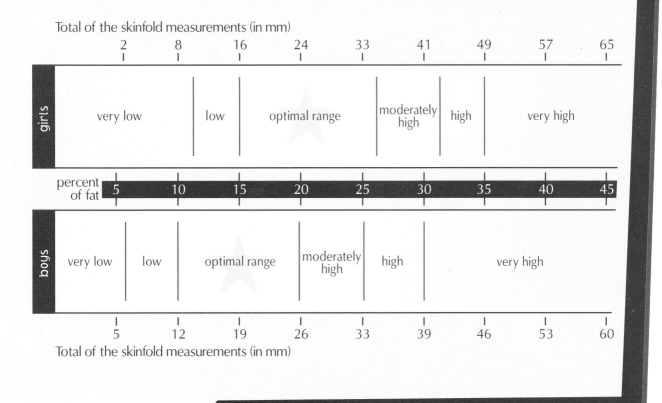

Agility Jump

Too much body fat is one factor that reduces agility. Being agile refers to your ability to change direction swiftly and easily. Agility is beneficial for many active games and sports, and it is often necessary for personal safety.

Tape a line on the floor and stand to one side of it. Keeping your feet together, jump sideways back and forth over the line as quickly as you can for 60 seconds. If your score is less than 145 jumps in 60 seconds, you need to work on becoming more agile.

Comprehension Checkup

I. VOCABULARY: Match the term with the body system(s).

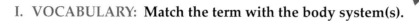

_M_	1. abdominals	_M_	21. hamstrings
_R_	2. alveoli	_S_	22. humerus
_C_	3. aorta	_E_	23. kidney
_C_	4. atrium	_R_	24. larynx
_M_	5. biceps	_S_	25. patella
_E_	6. bladder	_M_	26. pectorals
_R_	7. bronchi	_S_	27. phalanges
_C_	8. capillary	_D/R_	28. pharynx
_S_	9. carpals	_M_	29. quadriceps
_R_	10. cilia	_S_	30. sacrum
_S_	11. clavicle	_M_	31. sartorius
_S_	12. coccyx	_S_	32. scapula
_D_	13. colon	_S_	33. sternum
_M_	14. deltoid	_D_	34. stomach
_D_	15. esophagus	_S_	35. tarsals
_S_	16. femur	_S_	36. tibia
_S_	17. fibula	_R_	37. trachea
_M_	18. frontalis	_M_	38. trapezius
_M_	19. gastrocnemius	_C_	39. vena cava
_M_	20. gluteals	_C_	40. ventricle

C. circulatory
D. digestive
E. excretory
M. muscular
R. respiratory
S. skeletal

Do you know your anatomy?

II. SHAPING UP: Complete the puzzle to discover an important condition for good health.

1. light exercises before strenuous activity

2. the number of times a week you need aerobic exercise; at least _?_ times

3. the ability to move quickly and easily

4. two large organs in which the exchange of oxygen and carbon dioxide occurs

5. the ability to bend easily

6. a type of warm-up; lengthens your muscles, tendons, and connective tissue

7. the ability to keep on

8. how stretching makes you feel

9. most of it is stored in the subcutaneous layer of skin

10. a type of exercise that uses large amounts of oxygen; benefits the heart and lungs

11. the cardiac muscle

12. the amount of time needed for aerobic exercise; at least _?_ minutes

13. any physical activity

14. it increases the more muscles are used

15. being 20% or more overweight

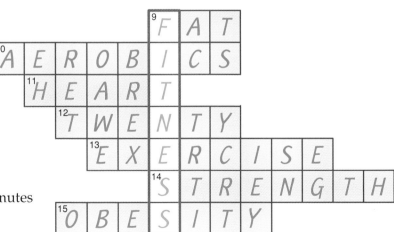

1. W A R M - U P S
2. T H R E E
3. A G I L I T Y
4. L U N G S
5. F L E X I B I L I T Y
6. S T R E T C H
7. E N D U R A N C E
8. A L E R T

9. F A T
10. A E R O B I C S
11. H E A R T
12. T W E N T Y
13. E X E R C I S E
14. S T R E N G T H
15. O B E S I T Y

III. A BONY BONUS: **Match each fact with its correct answer.**

_____B_____ 1. the number of bones in your body

_____C_____ 2. the amount of bones found in your foot

_____E_____ 3. where red blood cells are produced

_____F_____ 4. a cage that protects your internal organs

A. 226

B. 206

C. ¼ of the body's bones

D. ⅓ of the body's bones

E. bone marrow

F. ribs

G. skull

IV. WHO AM I? **Name the muscles.**

_____sartorius_____ 1. the longest muscle in your body

_____masseter_____ 2. a facial muscle that helps you chew

_____gastrocnemius_____ 3. your calf muscle

_____deltoid_____ 4. a muscle that helps you raise your arm

_____hamstrings_____ 5. located in the back of your upper legs

_____pectorals_____ 6. your chest muscles

_____quadriceps_____ 7. muscles in the front of your upper legs

_____diaphragm_____ 8. the muscle that causes your lungs to expand

_____abdominals_____ 9. muscles of the abdomen

_____Achilles tendon_____ 10. the tendon which connects your calf muscle to the back of your heel

V. A BENDABLE BODY: **Fill in the blanks. Then write the boxed letters in the corresponding boxes below to find out your body's framework.**

S I E R N U M   1. the breastbone

S K U L L   2. protects your brain

F E M U R   3. the longest bone

P H A L A N G E S   4. the finger and toe bones

P A T E L L A   5. the kneecap

T I B I A   6. the shinbone

F I B U L A   7. the calf bone

C L A V I C L E   8. the collarbone

C A R P A L S   9. the wrist bones

C O C C Y X   10. the tailbone

S C A P U L A   11. the shoulder blade

M E T A T A R S A L S   12. the long bones of the foot

V E R T E B R A E   13. help you stand straight or bend

H U M E R U S   14. a bone of the upper arm

1	2	3	4	5	6	7	8		9	10	11	12	13	14
S	K	E	L	E	T	A	L		S	Y	S	T	E	M

VI. **CATCH YOUR BREATH:** **Complete the puzzle. The terms on page 96 will help you.**

1. continuous exercises that help the body process oxygen

2. air sacs in the lung

3. the organ in which the exchange of oxygen and carbon dioxide occurs

4. the muscle which causes the lungs to expand

5. the hairlike structures in the air passageways

6. the two branches at the lower end of the windpipe

7. a growth of tissue at the back of the nasal passage which helps fight infection

8. a growth of tissue at the back of the throat which helps fight infection

9. a small bronchial tube

10. the windpipe

11. the throat

12. cavities in the thick bones of the face

13. the voice box

14. two words used to describe alveoli

15. another name for the pharynx

16. a tiny flap of cartilage that covers the trachea during swallowing

17. where food enters the body

1. A E R O B I C S
2. A L V E O L I
3. L U N G S
4. D I A P H R A G M
5. C I L I A
6. B R O N C H I
7. A D E N O I D S
8. T O N S I L S
9. B R O N C H I O L E
10. T R A C H E A
11. P H A R Y N X

12. S I N U S E S
13. L A R Y N X
14. A I R - S A C S
15. T H R O A T
16. E P I G L O T T I S
17. M O U T H

The Real You

There is more to you than meets the eye. When people see you for the first time, your appearance tells them something about you—but not everything. The real you is inside where no one can see.

What kind of person are you deep inside? The Bible says of Jesus' boyhood when He lived on earth, "And Jesus increased in wisdom and stature, and in favor with God and man" (Luke 2:52). Are you growing *physically* (increasing in stature)? To be the person God desires you to be, you also should be growing *mentally* (increasing in wisdom), *socially* (increasing in favor with man), and *spiritually* (increasing in favor with God).

Social acceptance— your friends are valuable

Not just skin and bones

Others around you do not see just a combination of body systems. They notice your smile—or lack of one. They notice how you sit, stand, and walk; what you are wearing; and if you appear well groomed. People judge you by your **appearance.** Do you go to school with a dirty neck, uncombed hair, clothes that look as if you had slept in them, and bad breath from unbrushed teeth? Your classmates may not enjoy being around you if you do.

The looking glass

Your posture often reflects the condition of your mind, revealing to others what you think of yourself. Tom felt self-conscious because he had grown so much taller than his classmates. He tried to make himself look shorter by slouching. Melinda showed that she did not have a good opinion of herself, because she let her shoulders and head droop and walked with her eyes downcast.

Good posture is important if you are to look your best. Not only is poor posture unattractive, it is harmful to your body as it forces your bones and organs into incorrect positions. When your posture is good, the parts of your body are positioned to do the work God designed them to do. Good posture allows your lungs to expand and fill with air. It helps your blood to circulate freely through your body, and it aids the digestion of food. Because your bones and good posture work together, it is especially important to have good posture when you are growing.

Stand and walk with your back straight, your head high, your shoulders back, and your abdomen in. Such posture will flatten your abdomen, lift your chest gracefully, and keep your shoulders from sagging and slumping.

Any movement of your feet and legs while you are standing for a long period of time helps reduce the strain on your circulatory system. When sitting properly with your back against the back of the chair, your body erect, and your feet flat on the floor, your body should align at right angles—chin, hips, knees, and feet. But good posture does not mean stiff, rigid posture. If you are sitting correctly, you should look and feel comfortable.

Japanese girls are taught to be graceful. They never stoop over to pick up an object but bend their knees instead, keeping their back straight. Such posture is better for the back than bending. This is also true when doing work such as gardening or even playing a game on the floor.

Smile protection

Being around someone with halitosis (bad-smelling breath) is unpleasant. Some foods, such as raw onions and garlic, may cause mouth odor, but the major cause of halitosis is mouth neglect. Cavities, gum disease, and mouth infections can all result in unpleasant mouth odor until they are corrected.

You can temporarily sweeten your mouth with a mouthwash or breath mint. But sugary breath mints form acid.

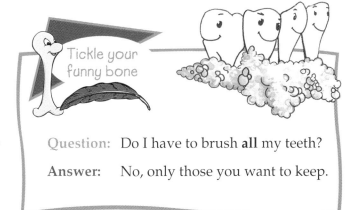

Tickle your funny bone

Question: Do I have to brush **all** my teeth?

Answer: No, only those you want to keep.

Plaque, a sticky, colorless film of harmful bacteria which is constantly forming on and between your teeth, adheres acids to the surface of your teeth, causing **dental caries,** or tooth decay.

The best way of dealing with halitosis is to practice good hygiene, including periodic dental checkups. Your teeth are one of the most durable parts of your body, but they are under continual attack. The time you spend daily on dental hygiene can ensure keeping them for a lifetime. You need to *brush your teeth as soon as possible after eating* to remove plaque and acid-causing food particles. Because plaque is forming continually in your mouth, you should brush your teeth at bedtime, too. You should also *floss your teeth at least one time every day* before you brush them. Flossing removes plaque and acid-causing food particles from between your teeth and near the gum line where your toothbrush cannot reach.

Some mouthwashes contain antibacterial substances to fight plaque. Other mouthwashes contain fluoride, a substance that helps teeth resist the

Give your mom a break—don't throw your clothes in the laundry hamper unless they are soiled.

destructive acids that plaque adheres to them. Fluoride is also added to many toothpastes. If you brush thoroughly with a fluoride toothpaste, you probably do not need a fluoride mouthwash unless your dentist recommends it.

Because straight, healthy teeth improve your appearance, they help you to feel confident. Do not keep them hidden. Smile—a winning smile.

The final touch

Your skin is like a coat of armor that keeps germs from invading your body and making you sick. It also protects you from injury, cold, and heat. But your skin is more than an amazing covering for your body; it is an important part of your appearance as well.

The best thing you can do for your skin is to keep it clean with soap and warm water. When you perspire, bacteria that are present on the epidermis combine with the perspiration to sometimes create a body odor. This is why it is important to *shower after vigorous exercise.* Parts of your body, such as your underarms, that are not exposed to air are especially vulnerable to body odor. Usually frequent washing with soap and water will control this. Some children your age (girls more than boys) need to use a deodorant or antiperspirant after washing to control perspiration in this area and to limit offensive odors.

Because the clothes next to your skin also become soiled from perspiration, oil, and bacteria on the epidermis, they

Question: What do skunks like best?

Answer: Being the scenter of attention.

Question: What do you call a messy, young kangaroo?

Answer: A sloppy joey.

should be changed daily to protect your body from diseases. Your outer clothing, however, can sometimes be worn more than one time before it has to be washed or cleaned. Your mother probably washes your clothes and keeps them mended, but it is your responsibility to help. Do you regularly hang up your clothes or fold them neatly when you change into play clothes after school? It takes only about one minute.

A daily bath (don't forget to wash your neck and fingernails!), clean clothes, brushed teeth, and combed hair will attract others to you instead of sending them away. It is a small price to pay for acceptance by others.

Quick Checkup
- ☐ I brush my teeth as soon as possible after eating.
- ☐ I brush my teeth at bedtime.
- ☐ I floss my teeth every day.
- ☐ I bathe or shower daily.
- ☐ I help keep my clothes clean and neat.

Who am I?

1. I often reveal what you think of yourself.
   posture

2. Mouth neglect is the major cause of me.
   halitosis

3. I am a film of harmful bacteria that constantly forms on your teeth.
   plaque

4. I am known as tooth decay.
   dental caries

5. I combine with bacteria on the epidermis to create body odor.
   perspiration

Your actions are showing

Good manners also help make you attractive to others—they make you pleasant to be around. And a knowledge of basic good manners gives you self-confidence. If you know what to say and do, you can relax and enjoy yourself. ***Good manners are a way of showing that you care about others.***

Everyday small talk

Do you enjoy talking to others? Good conversation is actually making an effort to give of yourself. Do you always speak clearly, pronouncing each word distinctly? If you need to, practice speaking alone with a clear, pleasing voice.

Whenever you are talking, look the person you are speaking to directly in the eye. If you are talking to a small group, move your eye contact from one to another so that everyone feels a part of the conversation.

Sometimes just giving someone a compliment can help start a conversation when you are with classmates you do not know very well. "Julie, I really like your patriotic poster. I'm going to try to be more original next year."

Remember that a polite person does not talk too much—being a good listener is important, too. Learn to give your full attention to the person who is speaking. Sitting or standing somewhat erect shows interest, whereas slouching shows rude indifference. And to interrupt or to walk away while someone is still talking is extremely thoughtless and rude. Whenever you listen with interest, it helps others to talk.

Do you ever look for something cheerful or kind to say to someone who is sad or is having a bad day? "That's such a pretty dress you are wearing, Cassie. The color is so bright and cheery." Even when you do not feel well, try to forget your troubles when you are around others. That will be giving of yourself in one of the nicest possible ways.

Quick Checkup
- ☐ I smile and say "good morning" to my teacher.
- ☐ I say "I'm sorry" if I hurt someone.
- ☐ I say "I'm sorry" whenever I am unkind.
- ☐ I say "excuse me" if I must walk in front of someone.
- ☐ If I interrupt, I say "excuse me" and let the other person continue talking.

Polite, proper, and pleasing

How do you treat other people? Are you kind to everyone you meet or just those you think are important? *One of the greatest tests of thoughtfulness is how you treat older people.* You should never contradict your parents, your teachers, or anyone who is older than you. It also usually sounds rude when you answer an older person by saying only "yes" or "no." How much more pleasant it sounds when you add some word or phrase or a person's name— "Yes, it is," "Yes, mother," "No, sir," "Yes, ma'am," "Yes, Miss Roberts."

Always call an older person by his or her full name rather than a first name. "Hello, Mr. Lowman. The flowers in your yard look pretty."

You should stand whenever an older person enters a room and stay standing until he or she is seated. Of course, you will want to give up your seat if few or no seats are left.

Do you think of others first or yourself first? *Loneliness is often a sign of thinking too much about yourself.* When you are busy doing something for others, you will no longer feel lonely. The result of thinking about others rather than yourself is a true graciousness that is seen by all around you.

Meeting new people

Introducing others. When you are making introductions, introduce a younger person *to* an older one, a friend *to* an out-of-town guest, a boy *to* a girl, a man *to* a woman, a person of no rank *to* someone who does have rank.

Do you know how to introduce your friend to your Sunday school teacher?

You should usually include both first and last names in an introduction. "Mr. Sellers, this is my friend, Jonathan Nipper. Jonathan, this is Mr. Sellers, the fifth-grade boys' Sunday school teacher."

You should not phrase your introduction as a command—"Pastor Cochran, meet my cousin Amy Stringer." It sounds much more courteous and friendly to say, "Pastor Cochran, this is my cousin from Idaho, Amy Stringer."

Sometimes you can add a few words of explanation which will give those you introduce something to talk about. "Lynne, this is Michelle Richardson, my classmate and neighbor. Michelle, this is Lynne Parker. Lynne just moved here; she's in the fifth grade, too."

Introducing yourself. When you introduce yourself to someone, simply say, "Hello, my name is Jennifer Hanowell." If you live out of town, you might include the name of your hometown in your self-introduction. "Hello, I'm Jennifer Hanowell from Sumas, Washington. I'm here visiting my aunt and uncle."

Proper responses. When you are introduced to someone, concentrate on the person's name. Then smile and repeat the name aloud as you say hello. "Hi, Mel, I'm glad to meet you" or "How do you do, Scott?"

Both boys and girls should stand when they are introduced to someone older. A boy should shake hands when he is introduced to another boy. When he is introduced to a girl or an adult, he should shake hands only if the other person offers his or her hand first.

The phone's ringing

Incoming calls. When the telephone rings, answer it as soon as you can. It is proper to say, "Hello, the Perry residence. This is Jon speaking." If your parents prefer you not to give your last name because of safety reasons, you might say, "Hello, this is Meggan," "Hello, Leann speaking," or "Good afternoon, this is Jason."

Quick Checkup

- ☐ I refer to an older person by his or her full name.
- ☐ I remember to introduce my guests to those they don't know.
- ☐ I use both first and last names when making introductions.
- ☐ I act as polite at home as I do away from home.

Courteous Conduct

Always shake someone's hand that is offered to you.

Courteous Conduct

"Please" changes a command to a request.

If you do not know who is calling, say "Just a minute, please" and get one of your parents. If the call is for your mother, put your hand over the mouthpiece and say, "Mom, it's for you." If your mother is in another room, say "Just a moment, please"; then lay the receiver down gently and go and tell your mother she has a phone call. If it will be a short time before she answers the telephone, let the caller know she is coming.

If you answer the phone and the call is for someone who is not home, ask to take a message. Be sure you get the name of the person who is calling and his telephone number. Repeat the telephone number to make sure you wrote it down correctly. If you are unsure of the caller's name, you may need to ask, "Could you spell your name for me, please?" Write the message carefully; then make sure that the person who was called gets the message.

Dialing out. When someone answers your call, say who you are and whom you are calling. "Hello, this is Nathan Witter. May I speak to Marty, please?"

If a stranger answers because you dialed the wrong number, apologize. "I'm sorry; I must have dialed the wrong number." Do not just hang up the receiver.

Quick Checkup

☐ I answer the telephone politely.

☐ I cover the mouthpiece before telling a family member that the call is for him or her.

☐ I write down telephone messages carefully.

☐ When making a phone call, I say who I am and whom I am calling.

For guests only

Be sure you get your parents' permission before inviting friends to your home. When a friend does visit you, make him comfortable and be sure you offer him your best. Remember, he is your guest.

When you are the guest, never grumble or complain and always be courteous so your host will want you back again. When you are leaving, be sure you thank your friend and his or her mother for the enjoyable time. If you stay overnight, or longer, at someone's home, it is necessary that you write a note of thanks to your hostess within a few days after the visit—unless, of course, your host and hostess are close relatives with whom you frequently visit back and forth.

Thoughtfulness counts

RSVP promptly. You may receive an invitation to a party or other special event with *RSVP* printed on the invitation. *RSVP* means "please reply"—you should call or write a reply within a few days of receiving the invitation so that the host or hostess knows how many people to plan for. If the invitation says *RSVP—regrets only,* you need to reply only if you cannot attend.

Written thank-yous. You should send a thank-you note or letter for every nice thing that is done for you within a week after the favor or gift is given. A written thank-you note is not necessary for presents that are given to you in person on

your birthday, Christmas, or other similar occasions. Saying "thank you" at the time the gift is received is sufficient. But it is always appropriate to send an additional note or letter of thanks if you wish to.

Quick Checkup

☐ Whenever I go to a friend's home, I thank my friend's mother for the nice time.

☐ If I receive a gift from someone, I write a thank-you note right away.

☐ I reply promptly to invitations containing RSVP.

Creative courtesy

Mrs. Peterson's students wanted to do something special for Mrs. Peterson when they learned that she was in the hospital for an emergency operation. David suggested that they all send a funny card to cheer her up and to let her know they missed her. Mandy had been in the hospital before, and she knew that cards are much more meaningful when they are unusual. She suggested that the class make a huge banner to place on the wall where Mrs. Peterson could easily see it. Mrs. Peterson was pleasantly surprised the next day with a big bright banner to hang on the wall facing her bed. Printed on the banner was the message—"WE LOVE YOU, MRS. PETERSON!" Surrounding the words was a display of homemade get-well cards, made and signed by each member of Mrs. Peterson's fifth-grade class.

Good manners include such things as sending cards, giving gifts, and doing nice things for people for birthdays or in times of sickness. Creative manners involve something extra. When you practice creative manners, you look for unnecessary or special things to do to make an occasion more meaningful for someone. The fifth-grade class would have expressed good manners by simply sending a card to Mrs. Peterson. But they expressed more love by using creative manners. Mrs. Peterson will probably remember the special banner and homemade cards made by her students much longer than she would remember a stack of ordinary get-well cards.

Healthful Hint

Add a friendly smile to common courtesy and you'll make many friends.

You can practice creative manners in many ways. You could give cards to friends for no special reason other than to say you care about them, or you could do the dishes for your sister when it was not your turn. You could help your mom or dad with some chore without being asked. Perhaps you could mow a neighbor's lawn for free while he is away on vacation. You could take some cookies to a shut-in, or offer to help care for your niece or nephew when your big sister is not feeling well. Creative manners involve showing love to others by cheerfully doing things they would not expect you to do.

The value of friends

We all need friends—life would be extremely lonely without them. But close friendships take time to develop. Have you ever gone to a new school without knowing anyone? It is hard to be the new boy or girl and have no friends. The Bible teaches that "A man that hath friends must show himself friendly" (Prov. 18:24). You cannot always expect others to show friendliness before you do. Sometimes you may have to take the first step to make friends. If you feel self-conscious, that is really a fear of not being accepted. You can overcome your self-consciousness by forgetting about yourself and thinking of others.

To have good friends, you must be a good friend.

subject immediately? A good friend cares about your deepest feelings. **Be a good listener.**

Do you always insist on doing what you want to do or on going where you want to go? **Be yielding.** Let your friends sometimes choose what activities you do—unless, of course, your friends want you to do something wrong.

Finally, be **loyal.** Do not forsake a friend when someone new comes along. Continue to be his or her friend even as you gain new friends. "A friend loveth at all times" (Prov. 17:17).

Choosing good friends

You usually choose friends who have interests similar to yours. Do you like sports? You will enjoy being with others who are involved with sports, too. Is reading your favorite pastime? You will enjoy being friends with another enthusiastic reader with whom you can discuss the books you read. Do you like to play table games, put together model airplanes, paint, or build things? No doubt you will choose friends who will join you in those activities.

Being a good friend

In order to keep friends, you must *be* a good friend. The apostle Paul gives us good advice on establishing lasting friendships: "Look not every man on his own things, but every man also on the things of others" (Phil. 2:4). In other words, **be considerate of others.** Take an interest in them. Try to imagine how your friend feels instead of considering only your own feelings.

How often do you listen to what your friends tell you? Really listen? A good friend listens and rejoices with you or tries to help. Have you ever told a friend something that was important to you only to have him or her change the

Quick Checkup
- ☐ I always try to be considerate of others.
- ☐ I am a good listener.
- ☐ I am cheerful.
- ☐ I never insist on having my way.
- ☐ I am a loyal friend.

Some friends may introduce you to new interests. Ericka usually had her nose in a book, but her new friend taught her origami [ôr′ĭ·gä′mē], the Japanese art of folding paper. Now they enjoy working together to make animals, flowers, and many other interesting objects. Pete was usually so involved in working on his stamp collection that he neglected physical activity until he made friends with Rod and joined his soccer team. A whole new world of interest opened up to Josh when he became friends with Kim, who had recently come from Korea. When Josh visited Kim's home he felt as if he had taken a trip to Korea. He even learned to say a few Korean words!

Be open to fresh ideas and new activities. Learn to know and enjoy a variety of friends. Share good times together with them. But because you are spending more time with your friends as you get older, it is vital that you have the right friends. No matter how much fun someone is to be with, if that person influences you to do wrong, do not choose him for a friend. Solomon warned young people: "My son, walk not thou in the way with them; refrain thy foot from their path: For their feet run to evil" (Prov. 1:15–16). Many young people have become ensnared by drugs and other evils because they chose the wrong kind of friends.

Healthful Hint

Never become close friends with those who do things you or your parents disapprove of.

Mental awareness—
your mind at its best

Keep on exercising

Just as your body becomes sluggish when it lacks regular exercise, so your mind needs exercise to be at its best. You exercise your mind through reading, studying, memorizing, and working out problems. *The more you think, the better you are able to think.*

Unlimited potential

Jan's computer can store records, alphabetize words, record phone calls, file information, address envelopes, write music, make posters, and perform many more tasks. Jan, however, uses her computer just for writing letters and research papers. She makes use of only about 5% of her computer's capabilities.

Although it is possible for the human mind to store millions of separate items, most of us use only a small fraction of our potential. Remember that the next time you feel you cannot work one more problem or read one more page. You can. God has given you a great capacity for learning. Maybe all you need is to take a deep breath and relax a minute. No one can destroy his brain through too much thinking. It merely becomes sharper with use.

When you were little, you read about the little engine that kept repeating while climbing a steep mountain, "I think I can, I think I can, I think I can," and he found out that he really could. If you approach your lessons that way, you will discover that you can do difficult things, too. The apostle Paul said it this way: "I can do all things through Christ which strengtheneth me" (Phil. 4:13).

Mind stretchers

Kathy saves one penny, nickel, dime, and quarter each day for 3 consecutive months. What is the greatest amount of money she could save if one of the months is February? *$36.90*

Andrew picked a basketful of apples. He gave 4 friends 4 apples each. Each time he gave apples to his friends, he ate one himself. If he has 5 apples left, how many apples did he pick? *25*

John wrote down two numbers. Their sum is 45; their difference is 3. What are the numbers? *24, 21*

If a month begins on Wednesday and ends on Friday, how many Thursdays are in the month? *5*

Dave collected 12 coins worth 75 cents. He has three times as many nickels as dimes. How many of each coin does he have? *3 dimes, 9 nickels*

Arrange six circles as shown. Move one circle so there are 3 rows with 3 circles in each row.

The world before you

Would you like to travel to the islands of Indonesia? Or to Israel where Jesus lived as a boy? Would you enjoy visiting a Russian family, wading barefoot through a rice paddy in China, or skiing down the snow-covered Alps in Switzerland? Do you dream of flying through space, visiting the planets? Or maybe your aspirations are not so high—you would love to go to a candy factory to see how they make your favorite chocolate bar! You can go on all these adventures and many more through reading.

Do you have a thirst for knowledge? Maybe you wish you could have known Abraham Lincoln, Hudson Taylor, Amy Carmichael, Babe Ruth. You can become well acquainted with these famous people through reading what has been written about them. There are treasures of knowledge in your school and public libraries. And the information you store in your mind each day will equip you for exciting opportunities that lie ahead.

Be on guard

John Bunyan, the author of *Pilgrim's Progress*, also wrote a book entitled *The Holy War.* In this allegory he portrays man's mind as a castle. Two powerful forces—God and Satan—compete for control. The main entrances to the castle are the eye-gate and the ear-gate. The army that is allowed to enter through one of these gates gains control of the castle—the mind.

Healthful Hint

Choose good books to read.

Your eye-gate

What comes into your castle (mind) through your eye-gate? What do you watch on television? Do you watch programs that are as contaminating to your mind as garbage is to your body? Perhaps the programs you watch portray harmful practices, such as smoking and drinking, as acceptable things to do. Perhaps they give you glimpses of violence or immorality. Satan loves to have you feed your mind such garbage, because he can use it to tempt you even weeks or months after the program is over.

What kind of books and magazines do you read? A Christian young man was trying to help other young people live for the Lord. He wanted to know what they were reading in order to show them the danger of it, so he read one of their dirty books. Afterward he regretted it. He could not forget the sinful acts he read about. Satan kept reminding him of them. "I wish I'd never read that book," he said. "I'll never do such a foolish thing again."

What kind of pictures do you look at? Ted Bundy, murderer of numerous women, testified just before he went to the electric chair that it was pornography (dirty pictures) that influenced him to commit his terrible crimes. He began looking at this kind of material when he was only a boy.

Protect your mind against such things. Can you say with the psalmist David, "I will set no wicked thing before mine eyes" (Ps. 101:3)?

Your ear-gate

Satan also wants to gain entrance into your mind through your ears. What kind of music do you enjoy? Listening to the syncopated beat of loud rock music not only impairs your hearing, but damages your mind as well. Many of the lyrics of popular songs today are inspired by Satan. They teach you to sin. They may encourage you to try drugs, to disobey your parents, to live selfishly, or to destroy yourself. Dirty jokes contaminate your mind, too. Be on guard at all times!

Establishing right attitudes

Has your mother ever said to you when you were behaving obnoxiously, "I don't like your attitude"? You know what she means, but do you know the definition of *attitude?* *Webster's New World Dictionary* defines it as "a bodily posture showing a mental state or mood; a manner that shows one's disposition." In other words, if you are yelling at your little brother, you are revealing your mental condition—what you are thinking and feeling.

Since *your attitude controls your actions,* it is important for you to know how to control your attitudes. And since *attitudes begin in your thinking,* it is necessary for you to know how to control your thoughts.

Paul teaches us that we are to think about things that are true, noble, right, pure, lovely, admirable, excellent, and praiseworthy (Phil. 4:8). These are positive thoughts. Often we think negative thoughts instead. We dwell on our troubles, our failures, the unkind things someone has done to us, our fears, our worries. These are unpleasant thoughts. They foster unpleasant attitudes that make us act in an unpleasant manner.

Healthful Hint

Consider the television programs you watch.

Do they help you think positive thoughts?

Guard your thoughts carefully!

Thoughts lead to attitudes, **attitudes** become actions, **actions** develop into habits, and **habits** form the **real you**.

Gratitude goes a long way

How is your attitude first thing in the morning? Do you always jump out of bed the first time you are called? Perhaps you sometimes find it hard to get up in the morning and face another day at school. Then it seems almost impossible for you to make your body do what you know you should do—get up quickly and cheerfully. Your mind immediately fills with negative thoughts: "My room is cold; I don't know what to wear; I don't feel like eating breakfast; I have a math test at school today."

Try applying this simple formula to improve your early morning attitude—"This is the day which the Lord hath made; we will rejoice and be glad in it" (Ps. 118:24). Start thinking about all the good things of your life and thank God for them. Can you walk? Talk? See? Hear? Read? Sing? Play sports? Do you have parents? Friends? A warm bed? Food? Do you know Jesus? Are your sins forgiven? Do you have eternal life? By the time you say "thank you" to God for these blessings that you usually take for granted, you will feel like a different person. And your family will be surprised at your cheeriness!

Quick Checkup

☐ I read at least one good book a week.

☐ I never listen to rock music.

☐ I guard my thoughts throughout the day.

☐ I begin each day with gratitude.

☐ I am a good example to others.

A school to be proud of

Your attitude at school makes a difference, too. When you are ready to graduate from high school, you will have spent well over 2,000 days in the classroom. These should be enjoyable days.

Making your school the best it can be requires your cooperation and your respect for those in authority over you.

Do you always display true Christian behavior? You are constantly watched by children in the lower grades. Are you an example to them for good? Or for not-so-good? Jesus said His behavior was an example for us: "For I have given you an example, that ye should do as I have done to you" (John 13:15).

Spiritual warfare—
your continuous battle

Remember that when Jesus was your age, He increased in wisdom (mental growth) and stature (physical growth). He also increased in favor with God (spiritual growth) and in favor with man (social growth). We have been discussing your physical, social, and mental development as you learn to relate to the world around you and the people in it. Now we will go a step further than gaining knowledge of the present world.

In the book of Proverbs, wisdom refers to God-given knowledge. Many people who have a great deal of knowledge about how to live in this world do not have wisdom. They do not know God. They relate only to the present, not to the eternal. Solomon tells us, "Happy is the man that findeth wisdom, and the man that getteth understanding" (Prov. 3:13).

God tells us in His Word that He loves us and sent His Son to die for our sins. If you believe in His Son and receive Him as your Savior, you become a part of God's eternal kingdom. Eternal realities—like God and heaven—sometimes seem unreal to us because we cannot see them with our physical eyes. Satan, our enemy, wants us to forget about them altogether.

Knowing your enemy

John Bunyan, who lived over 200 years ago in England, wrote an allegory to help people understand spiritual truths. His story, called *Pilgrim's Progress*, is about a man who journeyed from the

Healthful Hint

Solomon describes wisdom as better than rubies or anything else we might desire in this world.

City of Destruction to the Heavenly City. His journey pictures your life as a Christian on your way to Heaven. Part of this journey involves battling with Satan and his evil forces.

John Bunyan tells of Christian's stay at the Palace Beautiful on his journey. Christian slept in a room called *Peace,* for he had made his peace with God at the cross. He found out, however, that although a Christian has peace within, he has enemies without and must fight many battles.

You have experienced this, too. Even you who have received Jesus as your Savior find it difficult to always obey your parents, to always do what is honest and right, to live unselfishly every day. You keep sinning. That is because your old nature and Satan continually tempt you to do wrong. Remember that Satan is battling for your mind. He wants to control your thoughts, because then he will eventually control your actions.

Quick Checkup

Name the terms.

1. Increasing in stature
   physical growth
2. Increasing in wisdom
   mental growth
3. Increasing in favor with man
   social growth
4. Increasing in favor with God
   spiritual growth

Finally, my brethren, be strong in the Lord, and in the power of His might.

Put on the whole armor of God, that ye may be able to stand against the wiles of the devil.

For we wrestle not against flesh and blood, but against principalities, against powers, against the rulers of the darkness of this world, against spiritual wickedness in high places.

Wherefore take unto you the whole armor of God, that ye may be able to withstand in the evil day, and having done all, to stand.

Stand therefore, having your loins girt about with truth, and having on the breastplate of righteousness;

And your feet shod with the preparation of the gospel of peace;

Above all, taking the shield of faith, wherewith ye shall be able to quench all the fiery darts of the wicked.

And take the helmet of salvation, and the sword of the Spirit, which is the word of God:

Praying always with all prayer and supplication in the Spirit, and watching thereunto with all perseverance and supplication for all saints.

—*Ephesians 6:10–18*

Preparing for battle

At the Palace Beautiful Christian discovered the armory, a place where he could be equipped to do battle against Satan and self. Ephesians 6:13–18 tells about this armor that God has provided for Christian as well as for you: the armor that will protect you from Satan and his evil forces.

Your defensive armor

You are commanded to put on the whole armor of God—to put it on and leave it on. You should have every piece in place and never be without any of it.

A firm foundation. The first piece of armor is a *belt of truth.* "Stand therefore, having your loins girt about with truth" (Eph. 6:14). The loins (hip area) provide much of the soldier's strength during battle. This belt of truth which protects your loins is important in battle, because it holds much of the armor together. It is the foundation for other pieces of armor.

This firm foundation is the Word of God. In God's Word we find truth—truth about ourselves and about what God wants us to do. Everything we say or do should be according to the truth of His Word, and it should be done in His strength.

Vital protection. Because Satan often disguises lies as truth, you also need the remaining pieces of armor. Every soldier needs protection for the upper part of his body where such vital organs as the heart and lungs are located.

The protection that God provides—the *breastplate of righteousness*—is the

righteousness of Jesus. God demands righteousness of us because He is a holy God. But try as we might, we can never measure up to His requirements. He knows this, of course, so He arranged to *give* us this righteousness when we believe in His Son and receive Him as our Savior. "For He hath made Him to be sin for us, who knew no sin; that we might be made the righteousness of God in Him" (2 Cor. 5:21). He provided for our salvation. But it is not enough just to *have* the breastplate of righteousness; it must be *worn* in order to protect you against the temptations of Satan.

Always ready. Your next piece of armor is for your feet. A soldier needs durable shoes when he goes to battle—shoes that provide a firm footing, offer protection, and allow the soldier to move quickly.

The footwear God provides for the Christian—the *shoes of peace*—helps us across rough places in our pathway. Are your feet shod with the preparation of the gospel of peace? The word *preparation* means readiness. Are you always ready to tell others that God loves them so much that he sent His only Son Jesus to die for them? Isaiah said: "How beautiful upon the mountains are the feet of him that bringeth good tidings, that publisheth peace" (Isa. 52:7). The Christian who brings good tidings of what Christ has done has beautiful feet to those who hear his message.

Quenching fiery darts. The apostle Paul warns that Satan will throw flaming darts at you. These darts are temptations to make you sin. To ward them off you need a shield. God also provides you with this necessary piece of armor—the *shield of faith.* How can this shield help you when you are tempted? It brings God into your battle. The psalmist cried out, "The Lord is my strength and my shield; my heart trusted in Him, and I am helped" (Ps. 28:7). We cannot ward off Satan's flaming darts in our own strength, but as we trust in God—use our shield of faith—we can be victorious.

Assurance of future glory. We hear much these days about the importance of wearing helmets to protect the head from injuries. Football players and motorcyclists especially need them. Even bicyclists are urged to use them. God has provided a helmet for our spiritual battle, too. It is the *helmet of salvation*—*knowing* you are saved, being sure of it.

John Wesley grew up in a Christian home many years ago and eventually went from England to Colonial America as a missionary. Even though he worked very hard to teach God's Word, he was not sure of his own salvation. On his way back to England after his tour of missionary service in America, the ship he was on encountered a violent storm.

Wesley was terrified. He was not sure that he was saved. If he died, would he go to Heaven? He did not know.

On board was a group of Moravian Christians. They were not terrified of the storm as John Wesley was. Even the Moravian children were unafraid. They knew for certain that they were saved and would go to Heaven if they drowned at sea. John Wesley wanted this kind of assurance. Shortly after returning to England, a friend helped him receive it. It came when he realized that it was not by his efforts that he was saved but only by what Jesus had done for him. John Wesley spent the rest of his life traveling around England proclaiming this good news to people everywhere.

Your offensive weapons

Sharper than a two-edged sword. The armor we have been considering so far is defensive—armor to defend yourself from your enemy. God also provides *offensive* weapons. He gives His soldier a sword to drive the enemy away: a spiritual weapon for a spiritual battle. This first weapon, the *sword of the Spirit,* is the Word of God.

Jesus used this weapon against Satan when tempted in the wilderness. He said in answer to Satan, "It is written." All the authority of Heaven is behind God's Word that is written in the Bible. That is why it is so important for you to read and memorize it. It helps you to be faithful in learning God's Word if you can set aside the same time each day to spend with Him.

Quick Checkup

Name the armor.

1. Is the foundation for other pieces of armor
   belt of truth
2. Provides salvation through the righteousness of Jesus
   breastplate of righteousness
3. Brings peace
   shoes of peace
4. Quenches the fiery darts of Satan
   shield of faith
5. Gives assurance of salvation
   helmet of salvation
6. Is the Word of God
   sword of the Spirit/belt of truth

Healthful Hint

Underline verses or promises that have a message you can claim that day.

Memorize these to think about throughout the day.

Rom. 8:28
John 1:12

An upward appeal. The last weapon you have against your enemy is *prayer.* Do you make use of this weapon when Satan tries to discourage you or make you do wrong? When you talk to God you give Him a chance to help you. If you do not ask for His help, you will not receive it. What a privilege it is to be able to ask Him for whatever you need.

Before Christian left the Palace Beautiful to go on his way to the Heavenly City, he was given the belt of truth, the breastplate of righteousness, the shoes of peace, the shield of faith, the helmet of salvation, and the sword of the Spirit. His escort then introduced him to the secret weapon—prayer. He entered into a little room where he learned to pray to God.

The battle is the Lord's

As soon as Christian had left the Palace Beautiful he began to descend into the Valley of Humiliation. It was slippery and treacherous. To make matters worse, when he reached the bottom, he saw a horrible fiend coming toward him. He did not want to fight such a creature.

The fiend, Apollyon (another name for Satan), asked Christian where he had come from and where he was going. Christian replied, "I am from the City of Destruction, but have left that place to journey to the Heavenly City."

"Aha!" cried Apollyon. "I own the City of Destruction. You are a subject of mine. What do you mean by leaving my service?"

Christian bravely answered, "I was indeed in your service, but I found you were a hard taskmaster; and when I had a chance to escape, I took it gladly."

Apollyon then changed his tactics, asking Christian to return to his service and promising him a better time. When Christian stoutly refused, Apollyon tried to discourage him by reminding him of his past sins. Christian responded by quoting 1 John 1:9—"If we confess our sins, He is faithful and just to forgive us our sins, and to cleanse us from all unrighteousness."

Apollyon became furious when Christian quoted God's Word.

"I hate your Lord!" he screamed. "I hate His laws! I hate His people. I will not let you serve Him. I will kill you!" Rushing forward, he aimed a fiery dart at Christian's heart.

Christian raised his shield of faith, and the dart fell harmless to the ground. Apollyon continued to hurl his darts at Christian. The soldier defended himself valiantly at first, even making a few thrusts at his enemy with his sword. As the battle progressed,

however, Christian became weary. Apollyon finally lodged a dart just beneath the pilgrim's helmet and another above his shoe. As Christian began to lose blood, he grew faint. Apollyon, seeing his advantage, knocked the sword out of Christian's hand. Now he was defenseless. Or was he? Apollyon did not take into account Christian's secret weapon—prayer.

As Christian cried to God for help, he received strength to retrieve his sword and give Apollyon such a mighty thrust that the fiend cried out in pain and slunk away into the hills.

Does that describe the battles you have with the evil influences around you? Is it hard to go God's way when so many others are going in the opposite direction? It is hard but not impossible. "Be strong in the Lord, and in the power of his might" (Eph. 6:10). God has provided you with the necessary armor. If you stand firm and use it, Satan will flee from you.

Many Christians do not make use of their armor and weapons. They do not take time to read the Bible and learn God's truth. They forget to pray. Then they become an easy target for their enemy.

Quick Checkup

- ☐ I read God's Word daily.
- ☐ I memorize God's Word so I can avoid Satan's temptations.
- ☐ I talk to God about my problems and my joys.
- ☐ I watch for opportunities to tell others about Jesus.
- ☐ I know for sure that I am saved.

Comprehension Checkup

I. **KNOWING AND GROWING:** Complete the puzzle to find out what your thoughts, attitudes, actions, and habits form.

1. your body position when you sit, stand, or walk

2. they lead to attitudes

3. a way of showing others that you care; using good _?_

4. increasing in favor with God; _?_ growth

5. how to improve your early morning attitude

6. others judge you by it

7. increasing in favor with man; _?_ growth

8. a polite or loving action; another name for good manners

9. to grow mentally; to increase in _?_

10. how to protect your mind; always _?_ it

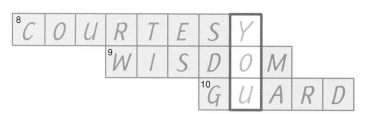

¹P O S T U R E

²T H O U G H T S

³M A N N E R S

⁴S P I R I T U A L

⁵R E J O I C E

⁶A P P E A R A N C E

⁷S O C I A L

⁸C O U R T E S Y

⁹W I S D O M

¹⁰G U A R D

Thoughts lead to attitudes, attitudes become actions, actions develop into habits, and habits form

T H E   R E A L   Y O U

II. **THE ARMORY: Match the armor with its function in the Christian life.**

_A_ 1. truth (God's Word)

_B_ 2. righteousness

_E_ 3. peace

_D_ 4. faith

_C_ 5. assurance of salvation

_A/F_ 6. Word of God

> A. belt
> B. breastplate
> C. helmet
> D. shield
> E. shoes
> F. sword

III. **EVALUATION**

1. Name two offensive weapons that help a Christian fight Satan's attacks.
   sword of the Spirit (God's Word, Bible) and prayer

2. Do you use these weapons daily?
   Answers vary.

Glossary

Pronunciation Key

Symbol • Example		Symbol • Example		Symbol • Example	
ā	āte	j	jog	sh	shark
â	dâre	ks	perplex (ks = x)	th	thin
ă	făt	kw	quart (kw = qu)	th	there
ä	fäther	ng	song	tṳ (cho͞o)	virtṳe
ə	ago (ə·gō′)	ō	ōver	*ū	ūnit
ch	chin	ô	côrd, taught,	û	ûrn
ē	ēven		saw	ŭ	ŭp
ĕ	ĕgg	ŏ	nŏt	zh	azure (zh = z)
*ẽ (ər)	pondẽr	oi	boil	′	little (lĭt′′l;
g	good	o͞o	bro͞od		shows that the
ī	īce	o͝o	bo͝ok		vowel is not
ĭ	ĭt	ou	out		sounded)

*Note: For simplicity, the alternate symbols are used for ẽr and tṳ.

Abbreviation Key

adj. adjective   *n.* noun   *v.* verb   *pl.* plural   *sing.* singular

abdomen (ăb′də·mən), *n.*
the part of the body containing the stomach, intestines, and other important organs

abdominal (ăb·dŏm′ə·nəl), *adj.*
of, in, on, or for the abdomen

abdominals *n.*
the muscles of the abdomen

absorption (əb·sôrp′shən), *n.*
the process by which food is made available to the body

Achilles tendon (ə·kĭl′ēz tĕn′dən), *n.*
the tendon connecting the back of the heel to the calf muscles of the lower leg

adenoid (ăd′n·oid′), *n.*
a growth of tissue at the back of the nasal passage that helps fight infection

aerobic (â·rō′bĭk), *adj.*
referring to the presence of oxygen

aerobics *n.*
a type of exercise which strengthens the lungs and heart; continuous activity without rest

agile (ăj′əl), *adj.*
able to move quickly and easily

alcoholic (ăl′kə·hŏ′lĭk), *n.*
a person dependent on alcohol

alimentary canal (ăl′ə·mĕn′tə·rē kə·năl), *n.*
the muscular tube through which food travels; includes the esophagus, stomach, small intestine, and colon

alveoli (ăl·vē′ə·lī), *n.*
air sacs in the lungs; *sing.,* **alveolus** (ăl·vē′ə·ləs)

anemia (ə·nē′mē·ə), *n.*
a condition in which the body has insufficient red blood cells

antibody (ăn′tĭ·bŏd′ē), *n.*
a protein produced by the body to help protect the body from disease

aorta (ā·ôr′tə), *n.*
the largest artery in the body

arteriole (är·tĭr′ē·ōl′), *n.*
a small artery

artery (är′tə·rē), *n.*
a blood vessel which carries blood from the heart

atrium (ā′trĭ·əm), *n.*
one of two upper chambers of the heart

attitude (ăt′ĭ·tōod), *n.*
the way a person feels about something; begins from thoughts

B-complex vitamins (bē kŏm′pleks′ vī′tə·mĭnz), *n.*
a group of water-soluble vitamins that help the body produce energy

bacteria (băk·tĭr′ē·ə), *n.*
microorganisms made up of one cell each; some cause infectious diseases

balanced diet (băl′ənst dī′ĭt), *n.*
a variety of foods containing all the nutrients necessary for good health

biceps (bī′sĕps), *n.*
a muscle at the front of the upper arm

bicuspid (bī·kŭs′pĭd), *n.*
a tooth having two points, or cusps, which function to crush food; located next to the cuspids

bile (bīl), *n.*
a greenish-colored substance produced by the liver; contains digestive substances and waste products

bladder (blăd′ər), *n.*
an expandable pouch containing liquid wastes

blood pressure (blŭd prĕsh′ər), *n.*
the force of blood (from the heart contracting) against an artery wall

bloodstream (blŭd′strēm′), *n.*
the blood flowing through the circulatory system of a body

body (bŏd′ē), *n.*
the physical part of man

body composition (kŏm′pə·zĭsh′ən), *n.*
the total of the fat and lean of which the body is made up

breathing (brē′ᴛᴴĭng), *n.*
the process by which air enters and leaves the body

bronchi (brŏng′kī), *n.*
the two branches at the lower end of the trachea (windpipe); *sing.,* **bronchus** (brŏng′kəs)

bronchial tube (brŏng′kē·əl to͞ob), *n.*
a tube branching from the bronchi

bronchiole (brŏng′kē·ōl), *n.*
a small bronchial tube

caffeine (kă·fēn′), *n.*
a substance that stimulates (speeds up) the heart and central nervous system

calcium (kăl′sē·əm), *n.*
a mineral contained in food and needed by the body; helps form strong bones and teeth

Calorie (kăl′ə·rē), *n.*
an amount of energy stored in food

cancer (kăn′sər), *n.*
a harmful growth that destroys healthy body parts

capillary (kăp′ə·lĕr′ē), *n.*
the smallest of the blood vessels

carbohydrate (kär′bō·hī′drāt′), *n.*
a nutrient that provides the main source of energy to the body

carbon dioxide (kär′bən dī·ŏk′sīd), *n.*
a waste gas that the body exhales (breathes out)

carbonic acid (kär·bŏn′ĭk ăs′ĭd), *n.*
an acid that helps transport carbon dioxide from tissues to the lungs

cardiac (kär′də·ăk), *adj.*
of, near, or affecting the heart

carotene (kăr′ə·tēn), *n.*
a nutrient which the body changes into vitamin A

carpal (kär′pəl), *n.*
one of eight wrist bones

cholesterol (kə·lĕs′tə·rol), *n.*
a fatty substance that is normally found in the blood, brain, nerves, and skin

cilia (sĭl′ē·ə), *n.*
the hairlike structures along the surface of the mucous membrane in the air passageways; *sing.,* **cilium** [sĭl′ē·əm]

circulation (sûr′kyə·lā′shən), *n.*
the continuous flow of blood through the body

circulatory system (sûr′kyə·lə·tō′rē sĭs′təm), *n.*
the body system consisting of the heart, blood, and blood vessels

cirrhosis (sĭ·rō′sĭs), *n.*
a buildup of scar tissue in the liver

citrus (sĭt′rəs), *adj.*
a fruit, such as an orange, lemon, or grapefruit, that is high in vitamin C content

clavicle (klăv′ĭ·k'l), *n.*
a collarbone

coccyx (kŏk′sĭks), *n.*
the tailbone

colon (kō′lən), *n.*
the large intestine

complex carbohydrate (kŏm·plĕks′ kär′bō·hī′drāt), *n.*
a long chain of sugars linked together

contract (kən·trăkt′), *v.*
to shorten or to become smaller

courtesy (kûr′tĭ·sē), *n.*
a respectful, considerate action

cranium (krā′nē·əm), *n.*
the eight flat bones of the skull that enclose the brain

crown (kroun), *n.*
the part of a tooth that can be seen above the gum line

cusp (kŭsp), *n.*
a point on the crown of a tooth

cuspid (kŭs′pĭd), *n.*
a tooth having one point, or cusp, which functions to tear apart food; located next to the incisors

defensive (dĭ·fĕn′sĭv), *adj.*
of or for defense (guarding against attack, harm, or danger)

deltoid (dĕl′toid′), *n.*
a large, triangular-shaped muscle of the shoulder; helps in raising the arm

dental caries (dĕn′təl kâr′ēz), *n.*
decay of teeth; cavities

dermis (dûr′mĭs), *n.*
the thick layer of skin beneath the epidermis

dextrose (dĕk′strōs′), *n.*
a form of sugar

diabetes mellitus (dī′ə·bē′tĭs mə·lī′təs), *n.*
a disease which causes unused glucose (sugar) to collect in the blood

diaphragm (dī′ə·frăm′), *n.*
a flat sheet of muscle that separates the chest cavity from the abdominal cavity; the movable floor of the rib cage that causes the lungs to expand

diastolic (dī′ə·stŏl′ĭk), *adj.*
the pressure of the blood while the heart is resting

digestion (dī·jĕs′chən), *n.*
the breaking down of food into a form the body can use

digestive system (dĭ·jĕs′tĭv), *n.*
the body system consisting of the teeth, esophagus, stomach, intestines, liver, and pancreas; the group of organs that breaks down and absorbs food

duct (dŭkt), *n.*
a tube in the body

dysentery (dĭs′ən·tĕr′ē), *n.*
a painful infection of the colon

ear-gate (ĭr′gāt), *n.*
an entrance to the mind through what is heard

endurance (ĕn·dŏŏr′əns), *n.*
the ability to keep on

energy (ĕn′ər·jē), *n.*
the ability to do work

epidermis (ĕp′ĭ·dûr′mĭs), *n.*
the outer layer of skin

epiglottis (ĕp′ĭ·glŏt′ĭs), *n.*
a tiny flap of cartilage that covers the trachea (windpipe) during swallowing

esophagus (ĭ·sŏf′ə·gəs), *n.*
a muscular tube connecting the pharynx (throat) and the stomach

excretory system (ĕk′skrĭ·tôr′ē), *n.*
the body system consisting of the kidneys and the bladder; the group of organs that helps remove waste products and helps regulate the amount of water in the body

exercise (ĕk′sər·sīz′), *n.*
any activity of the body

exhale (ĕks·hāl′), *v.*
to breathe out

eye-gate (ī′gāt), *n.*
an entrance to the mind through what is seen

facial (fā′shəl), *adj.*
of or for the face

fat (făt), *n.*
a nutrient which provides an extra supply of energy

fatigue (fə·tēg′), *n.*
physical or mental exhaustion

fat-soluble (făt′ sŏl′yə·bəl), *adj.*
able to dissolve in fat but not in water

fatty liver (făt′ē lĭv′ər), *n.*
a buildup of excess fat in the liver

femur (fē′mər), *n.*
the thighbone, or bone in the upper leg; the longest bone

fiber (fī′bər), *n.*
the rough parts of some fruits, vegetables, and grains that cannot be digested

fibula (fĭb′yə·lə), *n.*
the calf bone; the long, thin, outer bone of the lower leg

fitness (fĭt′nĭs), *n.*
the condition of being fit

flexible (flĕk′sə·bəl), *adj.*
able to bend easily

floss (flôs), *n.*
a thin, strong thread for removing food particles from between the teeth; *v.* to clean the teeth with dental floss

fluoride (flo͞or′īd), *n.*
a mineral which strengthens the enamel on a tooth

frontalis (frŭn·tăl′ĭs), *n.*
a facial muscle that raises the eyebrows

fructose (frŭk′tōs), *n.*
a form of sugar

gallbladder (gôl′blăd·ər), *n.*
a saclike pouch that stores bile

gastric juice (găs′trĭk jo͞os), *n.*
a digestive juice that softens food, kills bacteria, and starts digesting protein foods

gastrocnemius (găs′trŏk·nē′mĭ·əs), *n.*
the main calf muscle

glucose (glo͞o′kōs), *n.*
the kind of sugar used by the body for energy; blood sugar

gluteals (glo͞o′tē·əlz), *n.*
the muscles of the buttocks

goiter (goi′tər), *n.*
an enlarged thyroid gland causing a swelling in the neck

habit (hăb′ĭt), *n.*
something a person does without thinking about it

hair follicle (hâr fŏl′ĭ·kəl), *n.*
a little sac in the dermis (the middle layer of skin) in which the root of a hair grows

halitosis (hăl′ĭ·tō′sĭs), *n.*
bad-smelling breath

hamstrings (hăm′strĭngz′), *n.*
three muscles in the back of the upper leg

heartburn (härt′bûrn′), *n.*
a pain or burning behind the sternum (breastbone); caused when excess acid in the stomach is carried up the esophagus

heart rate (härt rāt), *n.*
the speed of the pulse

humerus (hyo͞o′mər·əs), *n.*
the bone of the upper arm

hydrogenated (hī′drə·jə·nāt′ĭd), *adj.*
combined with hydrogen (to form a solid fat)

hygiene (hī′jēn′), *n.*
cleanliness

immune system (ĭ·myo͞on′), *n.*
the body system that protects the body against disease-producing organisms such as bacteria and viruses; **lymphatic** [lĭm·făt′ĭk] **system**

incisor (ĭn·sī′zər), *n.*
a front tooth which functions to bite and cut food

infection (ĭn·fĕk′shən), *n.*
the result of being infected by pathogens (germs)

inhale (ĭn·hāl′), *v.*
to breathe in

insulin (ĭn′sə·lĭn), *n.*
a substance made in the pancreas which helps the liver store excess sugar

involuntary muscle (ĭn·vŏl′ən·tĕr′ē mŭs′əl), *n.*
a muscle that a person cannot consciously control

iodine (ī′ə·dīn), *n.*
a trace element found in the soil and ocean water; necessary for the thyroid gland to function properly

iron (ī′ərn), *n.*
a trace element that is recycled by the liver; necessary for the production of red blood cells

joint (joint), *n.*
a place where bones join

kidney (kĭd′nē), *n.*
one of two bean-shaped organs in back of the upper abdominal cavity; separates waste from the blood and sends it to the bladder

lactic acid (lăk′tĭk), *n.*
a waste that is formed in skeletal muscles during strenuous exercise

lactose (lăk′tōs), *n.*
a form of sugar

larynx (lăr′ĭngks), *n.*
the voice box

latissimus dorsi (lə·tĭs′ə·məs dôr′sī), *n.*
a triangular-shaped muscle of the back

ligament (lĭg′ə·mənt), *n.*
a band of tough fibers which joins bones to bones

liver (lĭv′ər), *n.*
the largest organ inside the body; has many functions relating to the digestive system

lung (lŭng), *n.*
one of two large organs in which the exchange of oxygen and carbon dioxide occurs

lung cancer, *n.*
a cancer that is most often caused by smoking tobacco

magnesium (măg·nē′zē·əm), *n.*
a mineral that the body needs more of when involved in long-endurance activities

malnutrition (măl′noō·trĭsh′ən), *n.*
poor nutrition

maltose (môl′tōs), *n.*
a form of sugar

manners (măn′ərz), *n.*
a way of showing that you care about others

marrow (măr′ō), *n.*
tissue in a bone that produces blood cells (red marrow) or stores fats (yellow marrow)

masseter (mə·sē′tər), *n.*
a muscle that extends from the cheekbone to the chin; helps the chewing process

mental (měn′t′l), *adj.*
of or for the mind

metabolism (mĭ·tăb′ə·lĭz·əm), *n.*
the process by which the body produces and uses energy from food

metacarpal (mět′ə·kär′pəl), *n.*
a long bone of the hand

metatarsal (mět′ə·tär′səl), *n.*
a long bone of the foot

mineral (mĭn′ər·əl), *n.*
an element, such as calcium, potassium, and magnesium, that is required by the body in small amounts and is found commonly in the soil

molar (mō′lər), *n.*
a tooth located in the back portion of the mouth that functions to grind food

muscle tone (mŭs′əl tōn), *n.*
the constant, slight contraction of muscle fibers in a skeletal muscle

muscular system (mŭs′kyə·lər), *n.*
the group of organs (muscles) used to move the body

nasal (nā′zəl), *adj.*
of the nose

nicotine (nĭk′ə·tēn′), *n.*
a poisonous substance in tobacco

nutrient (noō′trē·ěnt), *n.*
a substance in food that nourishes the body; necessary for proper growth and good health

obesity (ō·bē'sĭ·tē), *n.*
the state of being 20% or more overweight

occipitalis (ŏk·sĭp'ĭ·tăl'ĭs), *n.*
a muscle at the back of the skull

offensive (ə·fĕn'sĭv), *adj.*
of or for attack

oil (oil), *n.*
a liquid form of fat

orbicularis oculi (ôr·bĭk'yə·lâr'ĭs ŏk'yə·lī), *n.*
a muscle around the eye that causes it to close

organ (ôr'gən), *n.*
a body part made of living tissues that have a definite form and function within a body system

osteoporosis (ŏs'tē·ō·pə·rō'sĭs), *n.*
a disease in which the bones of adults become full of holes and are easily fractured

oxygen (ŏk'sĭ·jən), *n.*
a gas in the air that the body inhales (breathes in)

pancreas (păng'krē·əs), *n.*
an organ near the stomach that secretes digestive juices and hormones

patella (pə·tĕl'ə), *n.*
the kneecap

pathogen (păth'ə·jən), *n.*
a disease-causing microorganism; a **germ**

pectorals (pĕk'tər·əlz), *n.*
the muscles of the chest

peptic ulcer (pĕp'tĭk ŭl'sər), *n.*
an open sore in the alimentary canal

phalanges (fə·lăn'jēz), *n.*
the finger or toe bones; *sing.,* **phalanx** (fā'lăngks)

pharynx (făr'ĭngks), *n.*
the throat

phosphorus (fŏs'fər·əs), *n.*
a mineral needed by the body for making strong bones and teeth

physical (fĭz'ĭ·kəl), *adj.*
of the body

plaque (plăk), *n.*
a sticky, colorless film of harmful bacteria that constantly forms on and between the teeth

plasma (plăz'mə), *n.*
the liquid part of blood

platelet (plāt'lĭt), *n.*
tiny particles in blood which help blood to clot

posture (pŏs'chər), *n.*
the way the body is held while sitting, standing, or moving about

potassium (pə·tăs'ē·əm), *n.*
a mineral that aids the normal functioning of the nervous system and circulatory system

potential (pə·tĕn'shəl), *n.*
a capability or undeveloped ability

protein (prō'tēn), *n.*
a nutrient needed by the body for growth and repair

pulmonary (pool'mə·nĕr'ĭ), *adj.*
of the lungs

pulmonary artery (är'tə·rē), *n.*
the artery that supplies low-oxygen blood to the lungs

pulmonary vein (vān), *n.*
a vein that carries oxygen-rich blood from the lungs to the left atrium of the heart

pulse (pŭls), *n.*
the regular beating of the heart

quadriceps (kwŏd'rĭ·sĕps'), *n.*
a large muscle in the front of the upper leg

quench (kwĕnch), *v.*
to put out; to stop

radius (rā'dē·əs), *n.*
the shorter, thicker bone of the lower arm; on the same side as the thumb

respiratory system (rĕs'pər·ə·tôr'ē), *n.*
the body system consisting of the lungs,

diaphragm, bronchi, trachea, pharynx, and
nose; the group of organs that allows the
exchange of gases between the body and
the air

retrieve (rĭ·trēv′), *v.*
to get back; to recover

rickets (rĭk′ĭts), *n.*
a disease caused by a lack of vitamin D,
resulting in weak bones and deformities

root (rōot), *n.*
the part of a tooth which anchors the tooth in
the jawbone

RSVP, *v.*
please reply

sacrum (sā′krəm), *n.*
a thick, triangular-shaped bone at the lower
end of the spinal column

saliva (sə·lī′və), *n.*
a digestive juice in the mouth

sartorius (sär·tôr′ē·əs), *n.*
the longest muscle in the body; located in the
upper leg

saturated fats (săch′ə·rā′tĭd), *n.*
fats that are usually solid at room temperature

scapula (skăp′yə·lə), *n.*
a shoulder blade

sebaceous gland (sĭ·bā′shəs glănd), *n.*
a gland located in the dermis (the middle layer
of skin) that produces sebum (an oily substance); an oil gland

simple carbohydrate, *n.*
a short chain of sugars linked together

sinus (sī′nəs), *n.*
a cavity (hollow place) in the thick bones
of the face

skeletal (skĕl′ĭ·t′l), *adj.*
of the skeleton

skeletal system, *n.*
the body system consisting of organs known
as bones

skeleton (skĕl′ĭ·t′n), *n.*

the body's framework

skin (skĭn), *n.*
the body's covering

skin cancer, *n.*
a cancer caused by overexposure to harmful
ultraviolet rays; the most common form of
cancer

skull (skŭl), *n.*
the bones of the head; protects the brain

small intestine (smôl ĭn·tĕs′tĭn), *n.*
an organ of the digestive system in which most
digestion occurs

social (sō′shəl), *adj.*
having to do with getting along with others

soluble (sŏl′yə·bəl), *adj.*
able to be dissolved

spinal (spī′nəl), *adj.*
of or having to do with the spine or spinal cord

spinal column (kŏl′əm), *n.*
the backbone

spiritual (spĭr′ĭ·chōō·əl), *adj.*
of or for the spirit (not the body)

sternum (stûr′nəm), *n.*
the breastbone

stimulate (stĭm′yə·lāt), *v.*
to speed up

stomach (stŭm′ək), *n.*
an organ of the digestive system which pre-
pares food for digestion

strain (strān), *v.*
to injure or weaken by force; *n.* an injury to
a muscle caused by overwork

subcutaneous (sŭb′kyōō·tā′nē·əs), *adj.*
beneath the skin

subcutaneous layer (lā′ər), *n.*
the fatty layer of skin that stores energy

sucrose (sōō′krōs′), *n.*
a form of sugar

sunshine vitamin (sŭn′shĭn′ vī′tə·mĭn), *n.*
vitamin D; manufactured in the skin with the
aid of sunlight

sweat gland (swĕt glănd), *n.*

a gland located in the dermis (the middle layer of skin) that helps to control the body temperature and helps to remove excess body wastes

system (sĭs′təm), *n.*
a group of organs functioning together to perform a particular job

systolic (sĭ·stŏl′ĭk), *adj.*
the pressure of the blood while the heart is contracting

target heart rate, *n.*
the rate a person's pulse must reach and keep for 20 to 30 minutes in order to benefit his heart, lungs, and blood vessels

tarsal (tär′səl), *n.*
one of seven ankle bones

temporalis (tĕm′pə·răl′ĭs), *n.*
a muscle on the side of the skull

tendon (tĕn′dən), *n.*
a band of tough fibers that attaches muscle to bone

thyroid gland (thī′roid′), *n.*
a gland by the larynx that regulates the rate of metabolism (use of glucose) and the amount of calcium in the blood

tibia (tĭb′ē·ə), *n.*
the shinbone of the lower leg

tonsil (tŏn′səl), *n.*
a growth of tissue at the back of the throat that helps fight infection

trace element (trās ĕl′ə·mənt), *n.*
a mineral, such as iron, iodine, copper, manganese, or zinc, that is necessary in very small amounts to keep the body functioning properly

trachea (trā′kē·ə), *n.*
the windpipe

trapezius (trə·pē′zē·əs), *n.*
a large skeletal muscle that moves the scapula (shoulder blade)

triceps (trī′sĕps), *n.*
a muscle at the back of the upper arm

ulna (ŭl′nə), *n.*
the longer bone of the lower arm; forms the elbow at one end

unsaturated fats (ŭn·săch′ə·rā′tĭd), *n.*
fats that are usually liquid at room temperature

ureter (yo͞o·rē′tər), *n.*
one of two ducts (tubes) that connect the kidneys with the bladder

uvula (yo͞o′və·lə), *n.*
a small piece of tissue hanging down at the back of the mouth

valve (vălv), *n.*
a doorlike flap of tissue that opens and closes

varicose vein (văr′ĭ·kōs′ vān), *n.*
an enlarged vein near the surface of the skin

vein (vān), *n.*
a blood vessel that supplies blood to the heart

vena cava (vē′nə kā′və), *n.*
one of two large veins that enter the heart; *pl.* **venae cavae** (vē′nə kā′vē)

ventricle (vĕn′trĭ·kəl), *n.*
one of two lower chambers of the heart

vertebra (vûr′tə·brə), *n.*
one bone of the spinal column; *pl.*, **vertebrae** (vûr′tə·brā) help in standing and bending

villi (vĭl′ī), *n.*
microscopic projections in the small intestine; *sing.*, **villus** (vĭl′ŭs)

vital (vīt′′l), *adj.*
necessary for life

vitamin A, *n.*
a fat-soluble vitamin needed by the body for clear, smooth skin, strong nails, and shiny hair

vitamin C, *n.*
a water-soluble vitamin needed by the body to produce connective tissue

vitamin D, *n.*
the "sunshine vitamin"; a fat-soluble vitamin that helps the body absorb calcium

vitamin E, *n.*
a fat-soluble vitamin that helps prevent foods from being destroyed in the body by oxygen

vitamin K, *n.*
a fat-soluble vitamin that is necessary for the proper clotting of blood

voluntary muscle (vŏl′ən·tĕr′ē mŭs′əl), *n.*
a muscle that a person is able to consciously control

warfare (wôr′fâr), *n.*
a battle or conflict

warm-up (wôrm′ŭp), *n.*
a light exercise that increases blood circulation to the muscles

water-soluble (wô′tər·sŏl′yə·bəl), *adj.*
able to dissolve in water

wisdom (wĭz′dəm), *n.*
the quality of being wise; referring to God-given knowledge in the Bible

zinc (zĭngk), *n.*
a trace element that is necessary for normal growth, healing of wounds, and proper functioning of the immune system

zygomaticus (zī′gə·măt′ĭ·kəs), *n.*
a facial muscle that draws up the corner of the mouth when smiling or laughing

Index

Credits

Food items in photo montages throughout are by the publisher or taken from photo CDs by Corbis Images, Corel Corporation, and Digital Vision. Photos by the publisher are not credited. Abbreviations used: CC-Corel Corporations, CI-Corbis Images(Digital Stock), DV-Digital Vision, PR-Photo Researchers Inc., SS-Science Source, SPL-Science Photo Library.

Cover—children with father and in snow CI, vegetables CC; i—children with father CI, vegetables CC; 2-3 CI; 5—Dr. Tony Brain-SPL-SS/PR; 6—Don Fawcett-SS/PR, CNRI-SPL-SS/PR, CNRI-SPL-SS/PR; 12—Cecil Fox-SS/PR; 17—James Prince-SS/PR; 26-27—CI, sandwich CC; 28—Superstock; 42—U.S. Dept. of Agriculture; 55—Richard Heinzen/Superstock; 60-61 background CI, 60—Superstock, face behind digestive system throughout CI; 62—boy swinging throughout Superstock; 71—A. Glauberman-SS/PR; 76—Superstock; 88-89 background CI; 88—boys CI, ball and helmet CC; 92—Superstock; 97—face CI; 99—boy Superstock, cells Dr. Tony Brain-SPL-SS/PR; 101—Superstock; 102—CI; 120-121—field and boy CI; 122—Superstock; 124—Superstock; 130—Photri-Microstock; 135—Superstock; 141—CI; 146—CC.

Enjoying

Good Health

Science and Health

Science		Health
God's World	K5	
Discovering God's World	1	Health, Safety, and Manners 1
Enjoying God's World	2	Health, Safety, and Manners 2
Exploring God's World	3	Health, Safety, and Manners 3
Understanding God's World	4	Developing Good Health
Investigating God's World	5	Enjoying Good Health
Observing God's World	6	Choosing Good Health
Science: Order and Reality	7	A Healthier You
Matter and Motion in God's Universe	8	Let's Be Healthy
Science of the Physical Creation	9	Health in Christian Perspective
Biology: God's Living Creation	10	Managing Your Life under God
Chemistry: Precision and Design	11	Sex, Love, and Romance *(Sex Education from the Bible)*
Physics: The Foundational Science	12	

(9-12 bracketed for the last three Health titles)

Enjoying Good Health Teacher Edition

Second Edition

Editor: Naomi Sleeth

A Beka Book, a Christian textbook ministry of Pensacola Christian College, is designed to meet the need for Christian textbooks and teaching aids. The purpose of this publishing ministry is to help Christian schools reach children and young people for the Lord and train them in the Christian way of life.

Title page photos by Corbis Images and Corel.

Contents

Teaching Techniques

Enjoying Good Health

Enjoying Good Health emphasizes the importance of maintaining sound health habits. While reviewing the muscular and respiratory systems of the human body, each student is encouraged to measure his individual level of fitness. An in-depth study of the circulatory system adds to the student's knowledge of physical fitness. The study of nutrition focuses on the importance of a healthful diet and its effects on overall fitness and personal appearance. *Enjoying Good Health* also stresses personal responsibility in overcoming spiritual battles, concluding with a practical study of the Christian's spiritual armor.

Colorful art and photos excite interest, promote healthy relationships, and encourage the student to become physically fit. Beautiful, full-color illustrations of the body systems depict young athletes playing various sports. Healthful Hints help students to apply the concepts they learn to their own actions and encourage them to take more responsibility in caring for their body. Quick Checkups and Comprehension Checkups assist the teacher in evaluating comprehension skills and also promote the development of the student's thinking skills, while providing a thorough review.

Time Allotment

Enjoying Good Health is scheduled to be taught in lessons 133–171 in the *A Beka Book* Science Curriculum. (*Investigating God's World,* available from *A Beka Book,* is studied for the first 132 lessons). Science or health is taught daily for thirty minutes.

The text is read from and discussed each day. Quick Checkup questions are printed at frequent intervals throughout the text for immediate reinforcement of important concepts. To supplement the daily oral review planned by the teacher, a Comprehension Check is included at the end of each chapter for additional reinforcement.

Teacher Edition

This Teacher Edition contains the student text, answers to the textbook activities, the scope and sequence, and lesson plans for the entire course.

Tests, Quizzes, and Worksheets

Enjoying Good Health Tests, Quizzes, and Worksheets provides material for review and reinforcement as well as all of the written quizzes and tests to accompany *Enjoying Good Health*. The scheduling for tests and quizzes is given in the Scope and Sequence and Daily Lesson Plans which follow.

Grades are averaged at the end of each nine-week period (science the first three nine-week periods and health the last). In your grade book, record the grades of tests and exams in red ink and all other grades in blue or black ink.

Average a nine-weeks grade
in the following way:

1/4 Quiz average	96
1/2 Test average	95
(Count this average twice.)	95
1/4 Nine-weeks exam	+86
	372 ÷ 4 = 93

Health Teaching Charts 4–6

Health Teaching Charts 4–6 are designed for teaching and review. These large, colorful charts are labeled on the front for teaching and unlabeled on the back for review.

The Helicopter Bird Cassette

The Helicopter Bird cassette/booklet set features Uncle Bob Devine conducting exciting interviews. During the study of chapter 1, you may want to incorporate "S. A. Node" into the Daily Plans. The interview called "The Skin" would enhance the study of chapter 4. This cassette is available from *A Beka Book*.

Scope and Sequence

The following chart shows how to use *Enjoying Good Health* as an eight-week study.
In the Fifth Grade Science Curriculum, health is taught at the end of the year (lessons 133–171).

Chapter	Lessons	New Concepts/Charts	Tests/Quizzes
1 *Your Transpor-tation System* pp. 2–25	**1–8** (133–140 in the Fifth Grade Curriculum)	**Learn:** • to identify parts of circulatory system • about process of circulation • how to get proper rest • how to care for heart and other parts of circulatory system **Health Teaching Charts:** • Charts 13, 14	**Quiz 1** **Test 1** chapter 1 lesson 8 (curriculum lesson 140)
2 *Food for Vitality* pp. 26–59	**9–16** (141–148 in curriculum)	**Learn:** • to identify nutrients • how to establish good eating habits • about metabolism • how to maintain proper weight **Health Teaching Charts:** • Charts 1, 2	**Quizzes 2–3**
3 *Your 30-foot-long Canal* pp. 60–87	**17–25** (149–157 in curriculum)	**Learn:** • to identify parts of digestive system • about processes of digestion and elimination • benefits of drinking sufficient water • effects of emotions, caffeine, alcohol, and tobacco on digestion • proper mealtime etiquette **Health Teaching Charts:** • Charts 3, 4, 15, 16	**Quiz 4** **Test 2** chapters 2–3 lesson 25 (curriculum lesson 157)

Chapter	Lessons	New Concepts/Charts	Tests/Quizzes
4 *Physical Fitness in Action* pp. 88–119	**26–32** (158–164 in curriculum)	*Learn:* • how to exercise properly • about aerobic strength and endurance • to identify parts of respiratory system • to identify parts of muscular system • to identify parts of skeletal system • to identify parts of skin • about flexibility • about optimal ranges of fat content *Health Teaching Charts:* • Charts 5–16	*Quiz 5* *Test 3* chapter 4 lesson 32 (curriculum lesson 164)
5 *The Real You* pp. 120–155	**33–39** (165–171 in curriculum)	*Learn:* • how to have a healthy relationship with friends and acquaintances • how to properly care for personal appearance: hygiene, posture, smile • good manners • how to keep your mind active • how to establish right attitudes • how to be victorious in spiritual battles *Health Teaching Charts:* • Charts 5–16	*Quiz 6* *Test 4—Exam* chapters 1–5 lesson 39 (curriculum lesson 171)

Daily Plans

Chapter 1   Your Transportation System

Lesson 1: Life in the blood, pp. 3–6

Lesson Preparation

▶ Study: pp. 3–6/Lesson Development

▶ Write on the chalkboard (ckbd):
cardiac muscle, arteries, capillaries, veins, plasma, red blood cells, white blood cells, antibodies, platelets, iron, scab

▶ Display **Health Teaching Chart 13.**

Lesson Development

- **Introduction**

  1. "We are going to begin our study in health by learning about a very important transportation system. No, we won't be studying roads, buses, cars, or planes. We'll be learning more about the personal transportation system within your body. Have you ever wondered how blood, food, and oxygen get to the various parts of your body? Today we'll begin to find out."

     Show Health Teaching Chart 13. "God has given us a special system, the circulatory system, to transport the substances we need. The circulatory system consists of special blood vessels, blood, and a pump—the heart."

  2. Introduce the text—*Enjoying Good Health.*

     a. Call attention to title page/contents pages. Explain how to use pages and how they can be of great help. Then briefly explain features that are located throughout book—Your Amazing Body, Exercise 4 Fitness, Healthful Hints, etc.

     b. Have students find Glossary and Index at back of book. Briefly explain how to use each of these features.

     c. Have students open to chapter 1. Point out bold terms, Quick Checkups, and Comprehension Checkups that will be found throughout the book.

- **Instruction**

  3. Call on individuals to read pp. 3–6. Discuss the material, using terms from ckbd. Remind students that important terms in book are emphasized in bold print.

- **Reinforcement**

  4. Call on individuals to answer "Who am I?" questions from Quick Checkup on p. 6.

> **Homework (Hmwk):** Homework will begin in lesson 3.

Lesson 2: Your hardy heart, pp. 7–9

Lesson Preparation

▶ Study: pp. 7–9/Lesson Development

▶ Write on ckbd:
   cardiac muscle, atrium, ventricle, atria, valves

▶ Display **Health Teaching Chart 13.**

▶ Have a soft ball, bean bag, foam ball, etc., available.

Lesson Development

- **Review**

  1. Review material from lesson 1 by asking a question and then tossing a ball to an individual. If that student can answer question correctly, he quickly tosses ball to a friend who will answer next question. If any student answers incorrectly, he tosses ball back to you.

  Sample Review Questions:

  (1) What are the blood vessels that carry blood <u>to</u> the heart? *veins*

  (2) What are the blood vessels that carry blood <u>away</u> from the heart? *arteries*

  (3) What are the smallest blood vessels? *capillaries*

  (4) How much blood does the average child's body have? *3 quarts*

  (5) What percentage of the blood is made up of plasma? *over 50%*

  (6) Which blood cells carry oxygen? *red*

(7) Which blood cells fight infection and disease? *white*

(8) What helps blood to clot? *platelets*

(9) What does your body need to replace red blood cells? *iron*

(10) What is a blood clot on the skin? *scab*

- **Instruction**

  2. Introduce "Your hardy heart." Read/discuss pp. 7–9 (up to Quick Checkup). Each day, call on individuals to read the selected passage to class; use terms on ckbd as material is discussed. Occasionally, when time is limited, you may choose to read selected passages to class.

  3. Use Health Teaching Chart 13 to explain flow of blood through heart.

- **Reinforcement**

  4. Ask "Who am I?" questions from Quick Checkup, p. 9.

Lesson 3: Pathways through your body, pp. 9–17

Lesson Preparation

▶ Study: pp. 9–17/Lesson Development

▶ Write on ckbd:
  circulation, circulatory system, aorta, pulse, venae cavae, vena cava, varicose veins, blood pressure

▶ Have a watch with a second hand available for taking pulses.

▶ Display **Health Teaching Chart 14**

▶ Have **Anatomy Worksheet 1** counted out by rows
  for quick distribution.
    (Worksheets are in *Enjoying Good Health* Tests, Quizzes, and Worksheets. Answers are in the Test, Quiz, and Worksheet Key.)

Lesson Development

- **Review**

  1. Review by having several individuals name parts of heart as you point to them on Health Teaching Chart 14.

- **Instruction**

  2. Introduce "Pathways through your body." Read/discuss pp. 9–12, 16–17. Show students how to take their pulse.

3. Read/discuss "Target Heart Rate," pp. 14–15. Have students find their target heart rate by following formulas given on pp. 14–15. If possible, have students check their target heart rate after running in P.E. If not, encourage them to try it on their own at home.

- **Reinforcement**

4. Complete/check "Your Amazing Body," p. 13.

5. Complete and check **Anatomy Worksheet 1** as a class.

   Note: Throughout the year, be sure students correct any mistakes on worksheets so that they will have accurate information to use when studying for exams.

> Hmwk: Reread pp. 9–17. Answer Quick Checkup questions, p. 17, using complete sentences.
>
> > **Note:** Have students answer in complete sentences each time a Quick Checkup is assigned for hmwk.
> >
> > Give the hmwk assignment orally, being careful to speak clearly and slowly enough for all students to write it down accurately.

Lesson 4: Your body needs rest, pp. 18–21

Lesson Preparation

▶ Study: pp. 18–21/Lesson Development

▶ Write on ckbd:
   lactic acid, carbon dioxide

▶ Display **Health Teaching Chart 14.**

Lesson Development

- **Review**

1. Check Hmwk: Check Quick Checkup questions for completeness as individuals read questions and give their answers. Then collect hmwk for a more thorough check later.

2. Use Health Teaching Chart 14 to review parts of heart.

- **Instruction**

3. Introduce "Your body needs rest." Read/discuss pp. 18–21.

- **Reinforcement**

4. Have several individuals give good habits for restful sleep without looking on p. 21.

5. If time allows, have a quick contest to review pp. 18–20.
   Quick Contest Ideas: (1) boys answer first question, girls next;
   (2) first person in each row stands to answer first question,
   second person in each row answers next; (3) several students write
   answers to two or three questions at ckbd; then several more
   students come to ckbd, etc.

> **Hmwk:** Reread pp. 18–20. Complete the "Vocabulary" and
> "Identification" sections of Comprehension
> Checkup, p. 24.

Lesson 5: Protecting your heart, pp. 21–23

Lesson Preparation

▶ Study: pp. 21–23/Lesson Development

▶ Draw on ckbd:

Lesson Development

- **Review**
  1. Check Hmwk: Walk around room to check for complete
     hmwk as individuals read questions/give answers to
     "Vocabulary" and "Identification" sections of Comprehension
     Checkup, p. 24.

  2. Review the "Who am I?" sections in chapter 1.

- **Instruction**
  3. Introduce "Protecting your heart." Read/discuss pp. 21–23.

- **Reinforcement**
  4. Have individuals go to ckbd and write things that are good for
     the heart under the smile and things that are bad for the
     heart under the frown.

  5. Complete/check Quick Checkup, p. 23.

  6. Complete/check "Completion" and "Evaluation" sections of
     Comprehension Checkup, pp. 24–25.

Lesson 6: Review for Test 1

Lesson Preparation

► Study: Lesson Development

► Have **Quiz 1** and **Anatomy Worksheet 2** counted out by rows for quick distribution.

> (Quizzes are in *Enjoying Good Health* Tests, Quizzes, and Worksheets. Answers and suggested grading scales are in the Test, Quiz, and Worksheet Key.)

► Display **Health Teaching Chart 14.**

► Write each of the following terms on one side of a 4" x 12" piece of poster board and the definition on other side:

> *cardiac muscle, arteries, veins, capillaries, red blood cells, white blood cells, antibodies, platelets, iron, scab, atrium, ventricle, atria, valves, circulation, circulatory system, aorta, pulse, venae cavae, varicose veins, blood pressure*

Lesson Development

• **Review**

1. Give, grade, and collect **Quiz 1.**

   a. Say: **Prepare for a written quiz.** Teach students to quickly and quietly clear their desks and take out a pen and one blank sheet of paper for a cover sheet.

   > **Note:** Quizzes are scheduled at the beginning of the lesson, a day or so after the material is taught, with *no review* on quiz day. This procedure, which was recommended beginning in the spring of third grade, helps you to accurately evaluate the student's comprehension and retention of material being covered.

   b. Distribute Quiz 1. Have students answer all questions, being careful to keep their answers covered at all times. Walk around the room as students complete quiz.

   c. After students are finished, have them exchange papers (pass them forward one seat, back one seat, across, etc.) and take out a pencil. Tell them how you want incorrect answers to be marked, and then give correct answers.

   d. Have students write the number wrong at top of paper they are grading, compute the score, and return quiz to owner.

e. You may wish to train your students to call out their own quiz grades in alphabetical order for you to record quickly. Students could say "Question" if the quiz needs to be checked before the grade is recorded.

f. Collect papers; at a later time, check any questions and record those grades.

2. Complete/check **Anatomy Worksheet 2** as a class. Remember to have students correct any incorrect answers so that they will have accurate information to study for test.

3. Review circulatory system and parts of heart using Health Teaching Chart 14.

4. Play **Rows** using health flashcards made for this lesson. You may want to assign a name to each row to encourage enthusiastic participation from students: *Victorious Veins, Hardy Hearts, Prevailing Platelets, Winning White Cells, All-Star Antibodies,* etc. Have two rows compete against each other until all rows have had at least two turns. First student in each of two rows will stand to compete, then second student in each row, and so on until end of row. (Students not competing should answer questions in heads or on practice paper.) Hold up a card with definition facing students. First student to give correct term earns the chance to hold card. After every row has had two turns, have students with cards hold them up. Count/collect cards. Row with most cards wins.
   Note: You may want to interchange showing terms and showing definitions to help keep students on their toes.

Lesson 7: Review for Test 1

Lesson Preparation

▶ Study: Lesson Development

▶ Have flashcards prepared for lesson 6.

Lesson Development

• **Review**

1. Play **Around the World** using the health flashcards from lesson 6 to thoroughly review chapter 1. Start on one side of the room. Have one student stand beside the student seated behind him. Show a flashcard. The first students to answer correctly (either the one seated or the one standing beside him)

moves back to stand beside the next student. The other student sits in the desk. The object of the game is to defeat as many challengers as possible and to travel around the "world." The student who travels the farthest wins. Have all students return to their desks at the end of the game.

2. As time allows, play **Runs and Outs.** Divide class into two teams, the Runs and the Outs. Have the 1st member of each team stand; ask a question from chapter 1. If team member from Runs team answers first correctly, he earns one point for his team. If team member from Outs answers first correctly, Runs team has one out. Continue play until Runs have three outs. Then switch team names and allow former Outs team a chance to earn runs. Team with most runs at end of a designated time wins.

> **Hmwk:** Write definitions for these terms, using complete sentences: *arteries, veins, capillaries, scab, atrium, ventricle, blood pressure.* Study for Test 1: know bold terms in chapter 1, answers for each Quick Checkup, and answers for Comprehension Checkup. (If you are not sure about definition for a term, check Glossary, pp. 156–165.)

Lesson 8: Test 1

Lesson Preparation

▶ Have **Test 1** counted out by rows for quick distribution.
(Tests are in *Enjoying Good Health* Tests, Quizzes, and Worksheets. Answers and suggested grading scales are in the Test, Quiz, and Worksheet Key.)

Lesson Development

- **Hmwk Check**

    1. Quickly check terms for completeness and collect them. Go over them more thoroughly later.
    Note: On test days, hmwk check needs to be brief so that students have enough time to complete their test.

- **Test**

    2. Say: **Prepare for a test.** Teach students to quickly and quietly clear their desks and take out a pen and one blank sheet of paper for a cover sheet.

3. Distribute **Test 1.** Have students write their name and the date on test and then wait for instructions.

4. Go over the directions briefly.

5. Walk around room as students work. Check to see that each child is keeping all answers covered.

6. Collect tests; grade and record them later.

Chapter 2   **Food for Vitality**

Lesson 9: Full of energy, A balanced diet, pp. 27–31

Lesson Preparation

▶ Study: pp. 27–31/Lesson Development

▶ Write on ckbd:
nutrients, energy, balanced diet, carbohydrates

▶ If possible, bring in examples of carbohydrates such as bread, sugar, fruit, vegetables, etc.

Lesson Development

- **Review**
  1. Distribute graded tests and briefly go over them. Help students see areas where mistakes were made so that they can avoid making same mistakes on nine-weeks examination.

- **Instruction**
  2. Introduce "Full of energy" and "A balanced diet." Read/discuss pp. 27–29. Use examples of carbohydrates as you teach.

  3. Briefly discuss chart on pp. 30–31. Students will be using chart for homework.

- **Reinforcement**
  4. Ask several questions to review today's material.

> Hmwk: Read pp. 30–31. Use foods from Good Sources list to complete a sample menu—write what you would eat for breakfast, lunch, and dinner. How many different nutrients would you get from the foods you have chosen?

Lesson 10: A balanced diet (cont.), pp. 32–37

Lesson Preparation

▶ Study: pp. 32–37/Lesson Development

▶ Write on ckbd:
> *fats and oils, unsaturated, saturated, hydrogenated, protein, vitamins, water soluble, fat soluble, carotene, rickets*

▶ Make a chart with following information (on ckbd, poster board, or overhead transparency):
> *unsaturated fats—vegetable and fish oils*
> *saturated fats—animal fats, palm and coconut oils*
> *hydrogenated fats—many cookies, cakes, crackers, granola*
>   *bars, and candy bars*

▶ Make a chart of key terms to remember each vitamin (on ckbd, poster board, or overhead transparency):
> *Example:*
> *Vitamin D—"sunshine vitamin"*

Lesson Development

- **Review**

  1. Check Hmwk: Check for complete assignments while several students read their sample menus. Emphasize importance nutrients play in our growth and health.

  2. Ask several questions to review pp. 27–31.

- **Instruction**

  3. Introduce "Fats and oils," "Protein," and "Vitamins." Read/discuss pp. 27–31.

- **Reinforcement**

  4. Complete/check Quick Checkups on pp. 33 and 37.

Lesson 11: A balanced diet (cont.), pp. 38–41

Lesson Preparation

▶ Study: pp. 38–41/Lesson Development

▶ Write on ckbd:
> *minerals, calcium, phosphorous, osteoporosis, magnesium, sodium, potassium, trace elements, iron, anemia, iodine, goiter, zinc*

► Prepare flashcards (like ones prepared in lesson 6) for terms on pp. 27–41.

- **Review**

  1. Have several individuals give examples of the various types of fats.

  2. Ask questions to review material already covered in chapter 2.

- **Instruction**

  3. Introduce "Minerals" and "Trace elements." Read/discuss pp. 38–41.

- **Reinforcement**

  4. Complete/check Quick Checkup on p. 41.

  5. If time allows, have a quick contest using flashcards prepared for this lesson. (See lesson 4 for Quick Contest Ideas.)

Lesson 12: A daily food guide, Energy for activity, pp. 42–47

► Study: pp. 42–47/Lesson Development

► Write on ckbd:
  malnutrition, fiber, Calories, metabolism

► Have **Nutrition Worksheet 3** counted out by rows for quick distribution.

► Display **Health Teaching Chart 1.**

- **Review**

  1. Ask several questions to review vitamins and minerals from previous lessons.

  2. Complete/check **Nutrition Worksheet 3.**

- **Instruction**

  3. Introduce "Nutrients Your Body Needs," "Daily food guide," and "Energy for activity." Read/discuss pp. 42–46. Use Health Teaching Chart 1 during discussion.

- **Reinforcement**

  4. Quickly complete/check Quick Checkups on pp. 45 and 47.

  5. Play **Rows** to thoroughly review vitamins, minerals, and material covered in today's lesson. (See lesson 6 for game details; ask questions rather than using flashcards.)

Lesson 13: Eating balanced meals, pp. 47–52

Lesson Preparation

▶ Study: pp. 47–52/Lesson Development

▶ Have **Quiz 2** counted out by rows for quick distribution.

▶ Write on ckbd:
  Never skip breakfast!

▶ Display **Health Teaching Chart 1.**

Lesson Development

- **Review**

  1. Give, grade, and collect **Quiz 2.**

- **Instruction**

  2. Introduce "Eating balanced meals." Read/discuss pp. 47–52 (up to Quick Checkup). Use Health Teaching Chart 1 during discussion.

- **Reinforcement**

  3. Complete/check Quick Checkup on p. 52.

  4. Have a quick contest to review today's lesson as well as other material from chapter 2.

  > **Hmwk:** Reread pp. 47–52. Complete "Vocabulary" section of Comprehension Check, p. 58.

Lesson 14: Energy input/output balance, pp. 52–55

Lesson Preparation

▶ Study: pp. 52–55/Lesson Development

▶ Display **Health Teaching Chart 2.**

- **Review**

  1. Check Hmwk: Go over answers to "Vocabulary" section of Com-prehension Checkup as you walk around room checking for complete assignments.

  2. Review Food Guide Pyramid and daily food requirements using Health Teaching Chart 2.

- **Instruction**

  3. Introduce "Energy input/output balance." Read/discuss pp. 52–55.

- **Reinforcement**

  4. Complete/check Quick Checkup, p. 55.

  5. Complete/check Completion section of Comprehension Checkup, pp. 58–59.

  6. Have a **Row Contest** to review chapter 2. Have 1st person in each row stand. Ask a question; see which student answers correctly first. That student is seated and others remain standing. Continue until all students in one row have answered correctly; that row wins. Continue as time allows. (Make adjustments as needed so that all rows have same number of people.)

  > Hmwk: Reread pp. 52–55. Complete "True/False" and Evaluation sections of Comprehension Checkup, p. 59.

Lesson 15: Dodge Ball Run, Review, pp. 56–57

▶ Study: pp. 56–57/Lesson Development

- **Review**

  1. Check Hmwk: Go over answers to "True/False" and "Evaluation" sections of Comprehension Checkup as you walk around room checking for complete assignments.

- **Instruction**

  2. Introduce "Exercise 4 Fitness." Read/discuss pp. 56–57. If possible, play Dodge Ball Run sometime today.

- **Reinforcement**

  3. Play **Beat the Clock** to review chapter 2. Let each student answer one question as quickly as possible. Encourage students to answer in their heads if it is not their turn to answer aloud. Time the class to see how long it takes to go around the room; record the time. Make it a class goal to beat the record each time this game is played.

Lesson 16: Review of Chapter 2

Lesson Preparation

▶ Have **Quiz 3** counted out by rows for quick distribution.

▶ Display **Health Teaching Chart 2.**

▶ Prepare flashcards (like ones prepared in lesson 6) for terms on pp. 42–57.

Lesson Development

- **Review**

  1. Give, grade, and collect **Quiz 3.**

  2. Play **Popcorn** to thoroughly review chapter 2 (including Health Teaching Chart 2). Divide class into small groups. Make a statement for one group. If statement is correct, students in that group should remain seated. If statement is false, they should pop up quickly. Ask one student to tell why statement was false/ how it could be made true. Then continue with another group.

  3. If time allows, play **Tic-Tac-Toe** using the prepared flashcards.

Chapter 3   Your 30-foot-long Canal

Lesson 17: Digestion begins, pp. 61–65

Lesson Preparation

▶ Study: pp. 61–65/Lesson Development

► Write on ckbd:

alimentary canal, digestive system, incisors, cuspids, bicuspids, molars, wisdom tooth, saliva, salivary glands, pharynx, epiglottis, trachea, esophagus

► Display **Health Teaching Charts 3, 15.**

Lesson Development

- **Instruction**

    1. Introduce "Your 30-foot-long Canal." Read/discuss "Digestion Begins," pp. 61–65 (up to Quick Checkup), using Health Teaching Charts during discussion.

- **Reinforcement**

    2. Complete/check Quick Checkup, p. 65.

    3. Have individuals name teeth you point to on Health Teaching Chart 3.

    4. Ask several other questions to review today's lesson.

Lesson 18: A storage tank, pp. 65–67

Lesson Preparation

► Study: pp. 65–67/Lesson Development

► Display **Health Teaching Charts 3–4, 15–16.**

► Write on ckbd:
    stomach, gastric juice

► Have **Anatomy Worksheets 4–5** counted out by rows for quick distribution.

Lesson Development

- **Review**

    1. Use Health Teaching Charts 3–4, 15–16 for a quick review.

    2. Ask several other questions over pp. 61–65.

- **Instruction**

    3. Introduce "A storage tank." Read/discuss pp. 65–67.

- **Reinforcement**

    4. Complete/check Quick Checkup, p. 67.

    5. Begin **Anatomy Worksheet 4.** Students will complete worksheets 4 and 5 for Hmwk.

Hmwk: Reread pp. 65–67. Complete Anatomy Worksheets 4 and 5.

Lesson 19: Digestion continues, pp. 68–72

Lesson Preparation

▶ Study: pp. 68–72/Lesson Development

▶ Write on ckbd:
*small intestine, absorption, liver, bile, gallbladder, kidneys, bladder, cirrho-
sis, pancreas, insulin, diabetes mellitus, pancreatic juice*

▶ Display **Health Teaching Charts 4, 16.**

Lesson Development

• **Review**

1. Check Hmwk: Review material on Anatomy Worksheets 4 and 5
as you walk around room checking for complete assignments.

2. Ask several questions to review pp. 65–67.

• **Instruction**

3. Introduce "Digestion continues." Read/discuss pp. 68, 70–72.

• **Reinforcement**

4. Complete/check Your Amazing Body, p. 69.

5. If time allows, have a quick contest to review chapter 3 material
already studied. Include Health Teaching Charts in review.

Hmwk: Reread pp. 68–72. Complete Quick Checkup,
p. 72.

Lesson 20: Absorption and elimination, The importance of water, pp. 73–78

Lesson Preparation

▶ Study: pp. 73–78/Lesson Development

▶ Write on ckbd:
villi, colon, dysentery, caffeine, alcohol

▶ Display **Health Teaching Charts 15–16.**

- **Review**

  1. Check Hmwk: Go over answers to Quick Checkup as you walk around to check for complete assignments.

  2. Quickly review pp. 68–72.

- **Instruction**

  3. Introduce "Absorption and elimination" and "The importance of water." Read/discuss pp. 73–78 (up to Quick Checkup).

- **Reinforcement**

  4. Complete/check Quick Checkup, p. 78.

  5. Review by having individual students identify parts of digestive system as you point to Health Teaching Charts.

Lesson 21: Additional aids to digestion, pp. 78–81

Lesson Preparation

▶ Study: pp. 78–81/Lesson Development

▶ Write on ckbd:
  heartburn, peptic ulcer

▶ Display **Health Teaching Charts 15–16.**

Lesson Development

- **Review**

  1. Give a mini-quiz over pp. 61–77. Have students number from 1 to 3 on a scrap piece of paper. Quickly ask three questions. Then have a student call out all three correct answers while other students check their own work. Have students quickly number from 1 to 3 again and repeat exercise. Keep this review fast-paced and recognize students who answer all three questions correctly each time.

- **Instruction**

  2. Introduce "Additional aids to digestion." Read/discuss pp. 78–79.

  3. Read/discuss "First Base," pp. 80–81. If possible, play First Base sometime today.

- **Reinforcement**

  4. Complete/check Quick Checkup, p. 79.

5. If time allows, have a quick contest to review today's lesson. Include a review of the excretory system using Health Teaching Charts.

Lesson 22: Keeping mealtimes pleasant, pp. 82–85

Lesson Preparation

▶ Study: pp. 82–85/Lesson Development

▶ Write on ckbd:
   please, thank you

▶ Have **Anatomy Worksheet 6** counted out by rows for quick distribution.

Lesson Development

- **Review**

  1. Ask several questions to review pp. 78–81.

- **Instruction**

  2. Introduce "Keeping mealtimes pleasant." Read/discuss pp. 82–85.

- **Reinforcement**

  3. Complete/check Quick Checkup, p. 84.

  4. Complete/check **Anatomy Worksheet 6.**

Lesson 23: Review for Test 2

Lesson Preparation

▶ Have **Quiz 4** counted out by rows for quick distribution.

▶ Display **Health Teaching Charts 4, 16.**

Lesson Development

- **Review**

  1. Give, grade, and collect **Quiz 4.**

  2. Complete/check "Anatomy Pursuit," "Completion," and "Listing" sections of Comprehension Checkup, pp. 86–87.

  3. Play **Runs and Outs** to review chapter 3. (See lesson 7 for game details.) Include Health Teaching Charts in review.

Lesson 24: Review for Test 2

Lesson Preparation

▶ Display **Health Teaching Chart 2.**

Lesson Development

- **Review**

1. Check Hmwk: Go over answers to "Identification" and
   "Evaluation" sections of Comprehension Checkup, p. 87,
   as you walk around to check for complete assignments.

2. Play **Around the World** to thoroughly review chapter 2.
   (See lesson 7 for game details.) Include Health Teaching
   Chart in review.

3. If time allows, play **Beat the Clock** to review chapters 2 and 3. (See lesson 15 for game details.)

> Hmwk: Write definitions for these terms, using complete
> sentences: *villi, esophagus, cuspid, bicuspid, sa-
> liva, pharynx, absorption.* Study for Test 2: know
> bold terms in chapters 2 and 3, answers for each
> Quick Checkup, and answers for each Comprehen-
> sion Checkup. (If you are not sure about the defini-
> tion for a term, check Glossary, pp. 156–165).

Lesson 25: Test 2

Lesson Preparation

▶ Have **Test 2** counted out by rows for quick distribution.

Lesson Development

- **Hmwk Check**

1. Quickly check terms for completeness and collect them.
   Go over them more thoroughly later.

- **Test**

   2. Administer **Test 2.** Follow test procedures given in lesson 8.

Chapter *4*   Physical Fitness in Action

Lesson 26: Fitness factors, Aerobic endurance, pp. 89–95 (96)

Lesson Preparation

▶ Study: pp. 89–95/Lesson Development

▶ Write on ckbd:
   aerobic endurance, muscular strength, muscular endurance, agility, flexibility, body composition, warm-ups, respiratory system, aerobics

▶ Display **Health Teaching Chart 9.**

▶ Have **Anatomy Worksheet 7** counted out by rows for quick distribution.

Lesson Development

- **Review**

   1. Distribute graded tests and briefly go over them. Help students see areas where mistakes were made so that they can avoid making same mistakes on nine-weeks examination.

- **Instruction**

   2. Introduce "Physical Fitness in Action," "Fitness factors," and "Aerobic endurance." Read/discuss pp. 89–92.

   3. Read/discuss "Your Amazing Body," p. 93.

   4. Read/discuss "Fitness for a Lifetime," pp. 94–95. Encourage students to follow the directions for completing the chart in the next few weeks.

   5. Look at/discuss Respiratory system on p. 96. Use Health Teaching Chart 9 for a quick review.

- **Reinforcement**

   6. Complete/check Quick Checkups, pp. 91 and 95.

   7. Complete/check **Anatomy Worksheet 7.**

Lesson 27: Muscular strength and endurance, pp. (97) 102–105

► Study: pp. 102–105/Lesson Development

► Write on ckbd:
   physical therapist, sartorius, deltoid

► Display **Health Teaching Charts 7, 9–10.**

► Have **Anatomy Worksheet 8** counted out by rows for quick distribution.

- **Review**

  1. Use Health Teaching Charts 9–10 to review the respiratory system.

  2. Have a quick contest to review pp. 89–96.

- **Instruction**

  3. Introduce "Muscular strength and endurance." Read/discuss pp. 102–103.

  4. Look at/discuss Muscular system on p. 97. Use Health Teaching Chart 7 for a quick review.

  5. Read/discuss "Exercise 4 Fitness," pp. 104–105.

- **Reinforcement**

  6. Complete/check Quick Checkup, p. 103.

  7. Complete/check **Anatomy Worksheet 8.**

Lesson 28: Flexibility, pp. (98–99) 106–108

► Study: pp. 106–108/Lesson Development

► Write on ckbd:
   skeletal system, skull, ribs, sacrum, coccyx, red marrow

► Display **Health Teaching Charts 5–12.**

► Have **Anatomy Worksheet 9** counted out by rows for quick distribution.

- **Review**

  1. Reinforce muscle locations by playing **Simon Says.** Have students stand for this exercise. If a student uses an incorrect motion, identifies the wrong part, or moves when "Simon says" was not said first, he must be seated. Recognize individuals who stay in game longest.

     Sample Statements

     a. Touch your deltoid.

     b. Pinch your trapezius.

     c. Squeeze your biceps.

     d. Pat your triceps.

     e. Bend your abdominals.

     f. Put your left hand on your left temporalis.

     g. Tap your right hand on your occipitalis.

     h. Puff out your masseters.

     i. Point to your hamstrings.

     j. Massage your gastrocnemius.

     k. Sit on your gluteals.

     l. Squeeze your Achilles tendon.

     m. Move your orbicularis oculi.

     n. Rub your quadriceps.

     o. Touch your latissimus dorsi.

- **Instruction**

  2. Introduce "Flexibility." Read/discuss pp. 106–107.

  3. Read/discuss "Sit and Stretch," p. 108.

  4. Look at/discuss Skeletal system and Skin on pp. 98–99. Use Health Teaching Charts 5–6 and 11–12 for a quick review.

- **Reinforcement**

  5. Complete/check Quick Checkup, p. 107.

  6. Complete/check **Anatomy Worksheet 9.**

Chapter 4

7. If time allows, ask several questions (using Health Teaching Charts, if desired) over respiratory, muscular, and skeletal systems and over skin.

> **Hmwk:** Complete "Vocabulary" section of Comprehension Checkup, p. 114.

Lesson 29: Body composition, pp. (100) 109–113

Lesson Preparation

▶ Study: pp. 109–113/Lesson Development

▶ Write on ckbd:
  subcutaneous fat, obesity, triceps, gastrocnemius

▶ If possible, have skinfold calipers available for use.

▶ Display **Health Teaching Charts 13–14.**

▶ Have **Anatomy Worksheet 10** counted out by rows for quick distribution.

Lesson Development

• **Review**

1. Check Hmwk: Go over answers to "Vocabulary" section of Comprehension Checkup as you walk around checking for complete assignments.

2. Have a quick contest to review pp. 106–108.

3. Reinforce locations of bones by playing **Simon Says.**

   Sample Statements

   a. Wiggle your phalanges.

   b. Bend your carpals.

   c. Cross your tarsals.

   d. Touch your radius.

   e. Tap your ulna.

   f. Raise your right humerus.

   g. Pat your skull.

   h. Feel your clavicle with your right hand.

   i. Touch your scapula with your left hand.

j. Tickle your ribs with your phalanges.

k. Slap your left femur.

l. Cross your carpals.

m. Touch your patella with your elbow.

n. Rotate your tarsals.

o. Squeeze your humerus.

p. Place your phalanges on your sternum.

q. Lightly kick your tibia.

r. Point to your fibula.

s. Bend your vertebrae.

t. Sit and cross your femurs.

- **Instruction**

4. Introduce "Body Composition." Read/discuss p. 109.

5. Read/discuss "Your Amazing Body," pp. 110–111. Conduct activity to determine body fat percentages.

6. Read/discuss "Agility Jump," p. 112.

7. Read/discuss "Healthful Habits," p. 113.

8. Look at/discuss Circulatory system on p. 100. Use Health Teaching Charts for a quick review.

9. Ask to see how many students consistently reach their target heart rate while doing aerobic exercises.

- **Reinforcement**

10. Complete/check **Anatomy Worksheet 10.**

> Hmwk: Reread pp. 109–113. Complete Quick Checkup, p. 109.

Lesson 30: Review for Test 3

Lesson Preparation

▶ Have **Quiz 5** and **Anatomy Worksheets 11–12** counted out by rows for quick distribution.

▶ Display **Health Teaching Charts 6–16.**

► Draw on ckbd:

Trusty Teacher	Skillful Students

Lesson Development

- **Review**

  1. Give, grade, and collect **Quiz 5.**

  2. Check Hmwk: Go over answers to Quick Checkup as you walk around checking for complete assignments.

  3. Review human skin and muscles by completing/checking **Anatomy Worksheets 11–12.**

  4. Review body systems using Health Teaching Charts and playing a quick game of "What Am I?" Ask questions such as "I am part of the skin that acts as an insulator; what am I?" (subcutaneous fat) If student answers correctly, class gets a point. If student answers incorrectly, teacher gets a point.

  5. Complete/check "Shaping Up," "A Bony Bonus," and "Who Am I?" sections of Comprehension Checkup, pp. 115–116. (Students may need to refer to diagram, p. 97, while completing "Who Am I?")

Lesson 31: Review for Test 3

Lesson Preparation

► Display **Health Teaching Charts 6–16.**

Lesson Development

- **Review**

  1. Play **Simon Says** to review muscles and bones.

  2. Complete/check "A Bendable Body" and "Catch Your Breath" sections of Comprehension Checkup, pp. 117–119. Have students refer to pp. 96 and 98 and the Glossary as needed while completing the exercises.

  3. If time allows, use Health Teaching Charts to play **Around the World.**

Hmwk: Write definitions for these terms, using complete sentences: *warm-ups, aerobics, muscular strength, muscular endurance, subcutaneous fat, obesity.* Study for Test 3: know bold terms in chapter 4, answers for each Quick Checkup, and answers for Comprehension Checkup. (If you are not sure about definition for a term, check Glossary, pp. 156–165).

Lesson 32: Test 3

Lesson Preparation

► Have **Test 3** counted out by rows for quick distribution.

Lesson Development

- **Hmwk Check**
  1. Quickly check terms for completeness and collect them. Go over them more thoroughly later.

- **Test**
  2. Administer **Test 3.**

Chapter 5   The Real You

Lesson 33: Social acceptance—your friends are valuable, pp. 121–126

Lesson Preparation

► Study: pp. 121–126/Lesson Development

► Display **Health Teaching Charts 6–16**

► Write on ckbd:
  physical growth, mental growth, social growth, spiritual growth

T33

- **Review**

    1. Distribute graded tests and briefly go over them. Help students see areas where mistakes were made so that they can avoid making same mistakes on nine-weeks examination.

    2. Review body systems using Health Teaching Charts.

- **Instruction**

    3. Introduce "The Real You" and "Social acceptance—your friends are valuable." Read/discuss pp. 121–126.

- **Reinforcement**

    4. Ask several questions to review today's material.

> **Hmwk:** Reread pp. 121–126. Complete Quick Checkup on p. 126.

Lesson 34: Your actions are showing, pp. 127–137

▶ Study: pp. 127–137/Lesson Development

▶ Display **Health Teaching Chart 6.**

- **Review**

    1. Check Hmwk: Go over answers to Quick Checkup as you walk around checking for complete assignments.

    2. Ask several questions to review pp. 121–126.

- **Instruction**

    3. Introduce "Your reactions are showing." Read/discuss pp. 127–137.

- **Reinforcement**

    4. Have students practice introducing each other and answering the telephone.

    5. Briefly review skeletal system using Health Teaching Chart.

    6. If time allows, have a quick contest to review pp. 121–137.

Lesson 35: Mental awareness—your mind at its best, pp. 138–144

Lesson Preparation

▶ Study: pp. 138–144/Lesson Development

▶ Write on ckbd:

Your attitude controls your actions.
Attitudes begin in your thinking.

▶ Display **Health Teaching Charts 6, 16.**

Lesson Development

- **Review**

  1. Check Hmwk: Discuss with students results of their Quick Checkups. Encourage students to practice these actions and reactions until they become habits.

  2. Ask several questions to review pp. 127–137.

  3. Choose individuals to identify parts of skeletal and digestive systems as you point to them on Health Teaching Charts.

  4. Play **Simon Says** to review bones.

- **Instruction**

  5. Introduce "Mental awareness—your mind at its best." Read/discuss pp. 138–144.

- **Reinforcement**

  6. Have students complete Quick Checkup, p. 143.

  7. Review by asking several questions over today's lesson.

Lesson 36: Spiritual warfare—your continuous battle, pp. 145–153

Lesson Preparation

▶ Study: pp. 145–153/Lesson Development

- **Review**

  1. Have a quick contest to review pp. 121–144.

- **Instruction**

  2. Introduce "Spiritual warfare—your continuous battle." Read/discuss pp. 145–153.

- **Reinforcement**

  3. Complete/check Quick Checkups, pp. 146, 150, and 153.

  4. Ask several questions to review today's lesson.

  5. Complete/check "Knowing and Growing" section of Comprehension Checkup, p. 154.

Lesson 37: Review for Test 4

Lesson Preparation

▶ Have **Quiz 6** counted out by rows for quick distribution.

Lesson Development

- **Review**

  1. Give, grade, and collect **Quiz 6.**

  2. Complete/check "The Armory" and "Evaluation" sections of Comprehension Checkup, p. 155.

  3. Play **Beat the Clock** to thoroughly review chapter 1.

  4. Play **Around the World** to thoroughly review chapter 2.

Lesson 38: Review for Test 4

Lesson Development

- **Review**

  1. Play **Runs and Outs** to thoroughly review chapters 2–3.

  2. Play **Tic-Tac-Toe** to thoroughly review chapter 4.

  3. If time allows, play **Rows** to review chapter 5.

> **Hmwk:** List the armor each Christian should wear and what each piece represents. Study for Test 4, the nine-weeks examination: know bold terms in chapters 1–5, answers for each Quick Checkup, and answers for each Comprehension Checkup. (If you are not sure about definition for a term, check Glossary, pp. 156–165).

Lesson 39: Test 4

Lesson Preparation

► Have **Test 4** counted out by rows for quick distribution.

Lesson Development

- **Hmwk Check**

  1. Quickly check terms for completeness and collect them. Go over them more thoroughly later.

- **Test**

  2. Administer **Test 4.**

T38